Lunch with the Boss

To Joan
Sorry we missed
you. All the best.

Marni

Lunch with the Boss

Marni Blouin

HUNTER CARLYLE PUBLISHING

To my Boss,

Jack McQuaig

Order this book online at www.trafford.com/07-2677
or email orders@trafford.com

Most Trafford titles are also available at major online book retailers.

Note for Librarians: A cataloguing record for this book is available from Library
and Archives Canada at www.collectionscanada.ca/amicus/index-e.html

Printed in Victoria, BC, Canada.

ISBN: 978-1-4251-5913-9

*We at Trafford believe that it is the responsibility of us all, as both individuals
and corporations, to make choices that are environmentally and socially sound.
You, in turn, are supporting this responsible conduct each time you purchase a
Trafford book, or make use of our publishing services. To find out how you are
helping, please visit www.trafford.com/responsiblepublishing.html*

*Our mission is to efficiently provide the world's finest, most comprehensive
book publishing service, enabling every author to experience success.
To find out how to publish your book, your way, and have it available
worldwide, visit us online at www.trafford.com/10510*

Trafford PUBLISHING™ www.trafford.com

North America & international
toll-free: 1 888 232 4444 (USA & Canada)
phone: 250 383 6864 ♦ fax: 250 383 6804 ♦ email: info@trafford.com

The United Kingdom & Europe
phone: +44 (0)1865 722 113 ♦ local rate: 0845 230 9601
facsimile: +44 (0)1865 722 868 ♦ email: info.uk@trafford.com

10 9 8 7 6 5 4 3 2 1

About the Author

Marni Blouin is a speaker, writer, mother and wife. She is the founder of Blouin and Associates, a firm that specializes in Sales and Marketing.

After working in the corporate world for much of her youth, Marni's focus turned to raising her son, volunteering for the local school, fundraising and sitting on the school council. Once her family had grown she returned to the corporate world where she met Jack McQuaig.

Inspired by the work he had done over his lifetime and the work he continued to do, Marni was compelled to capture his life in this book.

The book, based on Jack's research and beliefs, will bring to all who read it the formula for staying mentally and physically fit into retirement years.

Published in 2004:   Hunter Carlyle Publishing
Suite 400, 229 Yonge Street
Toronto, ON M5B 1N9
Telephone: 416-941-9669
Fax: 416-941-9761

National Library of Canada Cataloguing in Publication

Blouin, Marni
   Lunch with the Boss :

ISBN 1-894584-17-1

   1. . 2. . I. Title.

Book Design: Karen Petherick, Thomas
Intuitive Design International Ltd.
Ontario, Canada
Text fonts: Goudy, Sanvito
Editing: Bill Belfontaine ·
Printed and Bound in Canada

Table of Contents

IN THE BEGINNING

I had been an "at home" Mom for 10 years and I wanted to get back into the work force. My son was in school all day and we needed more money. My situation was that I had become unhappy not contributing to the family financially. My husband did not want me to work as his job was extremely stressful and he wanted things to be taken care of at home and not have to deal with anything extra.

I applied for a few jobs and actually got them, but my husband explained that the little money I would make would be aggravating for him as he would have to pick up the slack at home in my absence. So I put it behind me and stopped looking.

Later in the year, a neighbor up the street from me came knocking on my door one bright morning. Molly and I had been members of the local welcoming committee for new people in the neighborhood and we had known each other for a few years. She explained that she was working for a man two days a week. His name was Jack McQuaig.

Molly now found that, as her children were now grown, she wanted more of a full time job and she had come to the end of where she could work with Jack's company. She wanted

1

to know if I would like to work one or two days a week replacing her in Jack's office. It sounded like a great opportunity to get me back into the workforce but not so demanding as to take me away from the things I had to do at home. I convinced my husband and he agreed that he could live with this arrangement. So I told Molly I would like to meet Jack for an interview.

Several weeks passed and then the New Year came. My relationship with my husband had become even more distant and I welcomed the call from Jack in January to go and have an interview in his Toronto office.

It had been a long time since I had worked and a very long time since I had been downtown. It seemed exciting and nerve-racking at the same time. Molly kindly offered to accompany me and show me the ropes of commuting again. When we arrived at Jack's office there were several people there, all from his other companies, and they were all watching me like I was from outer space.

I probably looked like I was feeling. My eyes were as big as saucers. Molly showed me into Jack's office and introduced me. He is a fairly tall man, with warm eyes and a welcoming handshake. His first words were, "Molly you didn't tell me this girl was good looking too!" I blushed, I was so nervous I wasn't sure what to do. Jack told me what he did and also explained some of his past accomplishments. It was all very new to me and not having been in the work force for awhile I didn't grasp the scope of what he was saying. It would become apparent to me as I grew to know Jack and his businesses.

My job was with his fourth company, Creative Communication Consultants. Jack had a full life in business and now semi retired wanted to focus on writing his books. I was given a McQuaig Word Survey, a tool that Jack created to help to appraise candidates for employment.

Jack got the results of my Survey and offered me my new career on the spot. I was thrilled.

Molly took on the task of training me, explaining that Jack only came into the office once a week, at lunch time. The rest of the week he worked from home. Molly would work diligently and report each week to Jack on what she was doing.

This job was to be one of the most rewarding experiences of my life and the beginning of *Lunch with the Boss*.

Chapter One

JACK'S PHILOSOPHY

It has been over seven years now that I have worked with Jack. In the first few years he would come into the office once a week and we would review the management strategies. However, it was a few years later that I learned to appreciate what an amazing man he is.

The first evidence of what a good boss he is happened one day when he was trying to give me another raise in salary. I was refusing the raise as I felt I was already well paid for what I was doing for one of Jack's companies, which was struggling to make a profit. Jack had been trying to give me another raise for some time and I had managed to talk him out of it. His new strategy was that I would have to take a raise or he would fire me. We both laughed at this being a new style of management but it convinced me that I was working for a very thoughtful and smart boss.

Other attitudes I noticed almost immediately was the way Jack interacted with his business associates and the kinds of policies he adopted which were very different from other firms for which I had worked.

One of Jack's secrets is that he likes people and tries to help them to be productive and happy on the job. Many bosses are more interested in making themselves look good. Jack's philosophy of management is that it is important to get the right people into the job, then coach them and guide them into doing good work. He often tells me if I hire good people it will make my job easy but if I hire weak people it will make my job impossible.

Psychological testing and good interviewing are his keys to appraising people. Once he hires the right person he will give that person authority and power to do the job his or her way, provided it doesn't conflict with company policy. If he or she isn't able to get results, Jack will continually counsel and coach and try to help that person.

If at this stage it doesn't seem to be the right fit, instead of firing the ineffective person Jack offers him or her free counselling by any consultant or psychologist who could help that person find a job.

He will give the employee six months to look for work for which he is well suited. Usually this results in having that person quickly find the right job, because Jack lets him go for interviews during working hours.

He calls this technique "firing a man or woman in such a way that they will like it". I must admit in the three small businesses owned by Jack McQuaig I have seen very little turnover.

Jack doesn't believe he can change people very much and always says that selection of the right personnel is the most important function of management.

People like Jack's style of management and they don't like to leave any of his organizations. I have worked for several other companies and I have found none that have the concern for people that Jack has.

Although he is really my boss, I don't feel like a worker, I feel like a partner and I have already been given some stock in the organization.

Every Saturday Jack and I get together for lunch at which time we discuss the business of the week and what we can do to improve it.

Jack knows what is going on in the business but he never tells me how to do my job. This gives me the feeling that I am in charge and it makes me want to produce. This all comes from the feeling that I am well liked and an important part of the organization.

Jack tells me that what little success he has is due to the fact that he doesn't work very hard and worries little about business. (I believe he loves doing his work so much he doesn't even realize that he is working). He delegates and gives people the chance to do their jobs. He claims that he is creative about the business and lets other people run it. However, when he delegates something, he does keep a string on it and follows up to see if the person doing the job needs help.

I believe one of the major reasons for his success is that Jack doesn't follow the crowd. He does it his way and is persistent in his beliefs. He once told me that if you visualize it, it will happen. Jack's philosophy is that any one can do anything if they put their mind to it. Part of that is visualizing the end result and working toward it. It is a philosophy I also believe in and have seen it work for both Jack and myself.

Another part of Jack's philosophy is the way he has of dealing with people. It is based on his belief that people don't change much as they go through life. If you can get their history you can predict how they are going to behave in the future. So when he interviews he doesn't concentrate too much on the personality, he concentrates on getting the history.

The history will also reveal the person's attitudes which are more important than aptitudes. The right attitude for the candidate is to want the job that will give him or her opportunity to show what he or she can do to produce results. The wrong attitude is to want the job because it pays well, has short hours and the work looks easy.

Jack believes that if a candidate has the wrong attitudes they will fail regardless of how good his or her appearance or whether you like him or her.

Another thing that won't show up in the interview, according to Jack, is motivation. The candidate will fail if he is lazy and yet there is nothing in the interview that will tell you about his motivation unless you get the history.

If he was well motivated in the past he is likely to be well motivated in the future, because he doesn't change very much as he goes through life.

Stability, maturity and aptitudes are other things which don't show up in the interview unless you know the questions to ask to get the history.

To find out how well motivated a candidate is Jack will ask him if he is a hard worker. If he answers "yes" Jack will ask him to give examples of any situations in which he has worked hard and Jack will judge his motivation by these situations.

Once he gets the right person on board, Jack delegates the work and gives that person authority and control over his work area.

Part of Jack's philosophy is that he follows certain rules in dealing with others and in coping with all situations that arise in his life, both personal and in business. He has spelled out these rules in his book *On the Path To Spiritual Fitness*.

His dedication to these rules and his belief in God have motivated him to create his own religion. He approves of all religions but couldn't believe in any of them so he created his own; Godliness. This religion has a great appeal for everyone because it gives the followers everything and demands very little in return.

According to Godliness there is no hell. There is no punishment. God doesn't punish you. If you do wrong, He will counsel you and help you to change your ways. In return all God asks of his followers is that they help their fellow men where possible and contribute something to any situation in which they are involved.

What I see is that Jack is a perfect follower of this religion and he tries to help others, who are struggling to believe in God.

In dedicating himself to this belief in God, Jack prays, meditates, chants, sings and affirms his belief constantly.

In my opinion his understanding and kindness come from his religious practice.

The other attitude that helps him is his humorous approach to life. He loves to laugh and my lunches with him are hilarious. He borrows heavily from the humour of George Bernard Shaw.

He sometimes practices Shaw's philosophy, "Anything for a laugh as long as it doesn't hurt anyone".

Jack isn't perfect but I will say he likes to live life with a light touch and makes few mistakes in his decisions.

I notice this in his dedication to golf, which is his big hobby. He believes golf can be a spiritual experience because it is played in a natural setting with hills and valleys and trees and flowers. He has written a book on golf entitled *Improve Your Golf with Spirituality.*

At the time Jack was writing this book, I had just taken up golf after 20 years absence from the game. Every Saturday and Sunday morning I'd type and edit the transcript and in the afternoon I would play golf. It was amazing, that as I read through and typed each word the book gave me a serenity that carried over onto the golf course. During that time, my game improved an amazing amount in a short time. I now will read the finished book before each season to remind me of the techniques that initially helped me so much. When I run into difficulty throughout the season, I again will turn to his book for help.

Jack also gives me copies of his subscription to Golf magazine so I can keep current with the suggestions of various golf pros. He always jokes on how good a golfer I am and how he has to practice to keep up. This is another example of the type of encouragement he gives people to keep them moving ahead.

Jack's business passion is public speaking. How did he get involved in this activity? He claims he was persuaded by one of his clients to speak at a convention. His speech was successful because he got a number of requests to do it in different companies. He liked it and began to promote his speaking activities.

This led to him speaking all over the USA and Canada.

There is hardly a city where he hasn't spoken for some organization. He was sponsored in most cities by The Sales and Marketing Executives Club, of which he was a member. He claims that his biggest day as a speaker was in San Francisco. He had 500 executives attending his seminar at the Mark Hopkins Hotel. In the audience were executives from the Los Angeles Sales Executives Club. They had come to San Francisco in 1958 to see if Jack was good enough to present his program *How to Pick Winners* in Los Angeles. After his presentation, these executives took Jack out to dinner and booked him to come to Los Angeles next year, which he did and had 600 in attendance

Chapter Two

ATTITUDES

In trying to give you a clear picture of what my boss is like, I have decided to describe his behavior in two areas, his attitudes towards life and people and his actual performance in different fields.

In this chapter I will describe his attitudes.

⤳●⤶

Getting along with people

When you first meet this unusual man you will feel that he wants to know all about you. He will soon get around to talking to you about your work and hobbies, your education, your family and friends. He is genuinely interested in learning everything about you and helping you to attain your goals.

If you are being introduced to him by one of his friends, he will likely get you talking about all areas of your life. This interest in you will make you feel good and quite important. To find out what you are really like he will probably ask for your opinion on different matters. You will be unaware that he is doing this because he avoids anything that would make you feel that you are being cross-examined. He does it in a subtle way and you are unaware that you are revealing many things about yourself.

What this tells you about him is that he likes people and is very interested in them. In spite of his liking for people he is not a person to become intimately involved with others.

I have often heard him say that he has few friends but he is close to his family members and has many interesting companions. In his book *On the Path to Spiritual Fitness*, he has described his formula for getting along with others.

You will soon notice humor in his light approach to life. He tends to see the humor involved in many activities which don't amuse others. I have often heard him say "Anything for a laugh." he'll soon get you laughing.

He loves to talk about humorous situations in which he was involved. For example one time at a meeting a man introduced him this way. "Jack McQuaig was born in Toronto, he has lived all his life in Toronto and we are looking forward to burying him here in Toronto." He likes to tell others this line.

He will talk openly about any humorous situations which happen in the family. For example one day his young daughter went to nursery school alone. She usually went with her mother. The teacher said, "Where's your mother, dear?" His daughter replied. "Daddy has been away for a few weeks and he came home this morning – so mummy is in bed playing with daddy."

Jack likes making jokes about himself. I've often heard him say "I don't have an enemy in the world, I've outlived them all."

Jack has many jokes and stories. There is never a time

that we get together that I am not entertained and educated at the same time. His approach to all subjects is serious but often he will make jokes to keep the conversation light. In the early days, this sometimes worked against him. People would tend to think he wasn't taking situations seriously enough. But I can assure you this was never the case. Humor is a way to relieve tension and laughing extends your life. I believe that these techniques have contributed to his longevity and success.

He often has a joke or two for me when I meet him. Sometimes they are new situations that have happened and some are old time favorites. I never tire of listening. After we have discussed our business, each week we usually touch on political subjects, economics and what is happening in our personal lives. Marriage often comes up as we have both been married twice. I like to bounce my thoughts off Jack to get his opinion. He once said to me, "A man is incomplete until he gets married. Then he is finished." We both laugh and move on to what we were discussing.

Here is another example of his modest approach to life. He sometimes starts a speech by telling that he is lucky to be married to a wonderful woman. She greets him every night when he comes home with two gin martinis and she drinks them both. She says she needs two martinis to get through an evening with him.

Even though Jack jokes, there is always a connection to what we are talking about. The lessons in the jokes are as valid as the serious parts of our conversation. He tells stories that make fun of his shortcomings. This relaxes people and makes them feel at ease.

Being Spiritual

You don't have to know my boss very long before you find out that he is a very spiritual person.

He has recently written a book entitled *Eustress, the secret of Success and Happiness.*

He started the book by writing in the preface that the first step in getting rid of distress is to pray and ask for God's help. God can do anything including relieving you of distress.

This is typical of Jack's way of thinking and acting. His big goal in life is to get so connected with God and the spiritual that he will have God's presence in every thought he thinks and every act he performs. I believe that Jack practices his spirituality in very practical ways.

One day at the Arts and Letters Club a man criticized him for monopolizing the time of the speakers at luncheon meetings.

Jack knew many of the speakers and they would all want to talk with him. He was thinking of complaining to this man about his criticism. But after thinking of what the spiritual person would do he changed his attitude and spoke to the man in a positive way.

He said, "Harry, thanks for alerting me to this apparently selfish act of mine in talking to our speakers. The problem is that I know many of these people and they want to talk with me."

After this conversation, Harry changed his attitude completely and he and Jack became friends.

Giving

My boss enjoys giving things to people. For example, he has written twelve books and he gives most of them to people whom he thinks are in need of the message in the book.

He has written the book, *Yes, You Can Quit Smoking*, to try and save the lives of people who smoke. He gives the book to smokers and to people who have friends and relatives who smoke.

Every time we meet for lunch I carry an extra book with me in case we run into someone new to whom Jack has not given a book. All of the staff at the restaurants greet Jack warmly and respectfully. Always interested in how he is doing and what new joke he has ready to make them laugh.

One young lady didn't smoke but she had two friends that did. Jack gave her the book, which she gave to her friends and they both quit smoking. I love it when he endorses a book. People wait patiently for him to write and he always has a phrase or a statement about the person that makes them feel important.

Often Jack will pick up the tab for everyone when he is out for dinner. I know of one occasion where he was at a table with six people. Two of these people were friends of Jack, the other three were strangers to him and although everyone was expected to pay their own way Jack picked up the bill for everybody. He loves giving to people and making them happy.

The tip is a way of helping waiters and waitresses. Jack was having lunch one day with two of his clients who urged him not to tip on the tax to which Jack replied, " I am not trying to lower my tip I am trying to raise it because these waiters need money more than I do". That is the way Jack is. He believes he is very lucky. He remembers what it was like to struggle and not have any money and he never forgets that others do not have as much as he does now. He usually tips 20 to 25 per cent of the total bill.

Several weeks later he was having lunch with the same two clients and when he asked for the check the waiter said, "There is no check to-day. You have been giving me big tips and I want to repay you." People want to repay Jack for his generosity.

With regard to income tax he doesn't try to avoid it because the government needs money to build roads and bridges and to improve the street lighting etc.

Jack decided a few years ago that he wanted to take singing lessons. He met a woman who sang in the church choir and was a teacher and they agreed on a time to meet each week. Jack was thrilled and so began his lessons. They were trying to agree on a price per half hour to pay her. The teacher only wanted twenty dollars. Jack was concerned that this was not enough.

The next time we met for lunch Jack asked my opinion on what I thought singing lessons would cost. After some conversation and comparison to other lessons I have had in other areas, Jack concluded that $30 was about right for a half hour lesson. He originally wanted to pay $50. The conscientious young teacher immediately said no to that. But Jack's persuasive manner won her over and they compromised and settled on $30 as a fee for half an hour.

Another passion of Jack's is art. Some years ago he was buying the art of young painters. His plan was to pay them for their art and then have cocktail parties for business executives and try to sell them the art of these struggling young painters. Once he was faced with a young conscientious person who was trying to sell his art for twenty-five dollars. Jack couldn't agree to this. He knew the man was struggling and also knew the time and money it takes to paint a picture. Jack told the artist he would pay no less than $50 per piece. The young man was thrilled. Unfortunately, with all of Jack's business and the pressures of family life, he was not able to sell the art of the young painters. The art still hangs in his offices in Toronto.

There are so many examples of Jack's generosity. I could go on and on but these examples will give you the essence of what he is like.

Leading

The first sign that Jack was a leader came in his early days when he was captain of playground hockey teams. The next situation, in which he revealed some talent for leadership ability, was at Queen's University.

When he attended Queens to take a Bachelor of Commerce degree, he was a member of the Commerce Club, which automatically included all four years of the commerce course.

Jack was first elected to the Board of Directors and later to be president of the Club. This gave him some good practice in public speaking because he had to introduce and thank high-level academic speakers who presented programs at the Club.

Later when he joined the Toronto Arts and Letters Club he was appointed chairman of the Writers Table, which is an organization within the club which invites writers to speak to twenty or thirty people who want to become writers. Here again he gets much practice in introducing and thanking speakers.

The membership of The Rotary Club of Toronto is made up of approximately three hundred top executives from the city. Every Friday at lunch the Club has a high profile speaker come to keep the members up to date on new ideas and new ways in which they can improve the environment of the City and help the underprivileged. Jack has been the guest speaker at the Friday luncheons on three occasions.

The Rotary Club is an organization which tries to improve the city or town where it is located and it is constantly urging its members to work harder for the underprivileged.

Jack felt that many of the members were overworked and should not be urged to work any harder. However he felt that they could all work smarter. As a result of his analysis he got approval from the Club to start a forum to bring to the Rotary members new ideas and new ways to keep healthy and productive.

For approximately ten years Jack conducted these forum meetings every Friday before the Rotary luncheon. A few dedicated members attended these meetings but unfortunately it did not catch on in the big way it deserved and was abandoned by the Club after about ten years.

Jack was very frustrated about this because he felt it was a very fine way to keep the Rotarians up to date so they could work smarter instead of harder. Because of his persistence he hasn't given up on this, instead he plans to approach it in a different way.

Jack joined the Sales and Marketing Executives Club in his early business days. Soon he was on the board of directors and later was asked to be the president of the club, which job he refused because of a heavy work load.

Persisting

The first example of his persistence was about the raise he continually tried to give me as I mentioned in the beginning of the book. I have often heard Jack say that persistence is just as important as talent. He claims that many people have great talents which go unrecognized because they give up too soon. When their manuscript is returned by one or two publishers they are hurt and stop sending it to any other organization that might publish it. Jack never stops trying, either personally or professionally to achieve his goals.

In learning to play golf he became very frustrated but he kept practicing and taking lessons and finally he learned enough about the game to write his book on golf, *Improve Your Golf with Spirituality*. Even today Jack spends 2 or 3 days a week at his golf club chipping and putting to keep up his game.

When Jack began speaking professionally, he hired a voice coach and he started looking at other professional speakers and paying attention to the clothes they wore and how they handled themselves. He is continually trying new things to improve his speeches and presentations.

Attitudes

Being Spiritual

At Queen's University Jack played on the junior hockey team and he also did much socializing and going to parties. Near the end of his final year, he had to cram if he was going to pass his exams. He gave up all other activities, drank a lot of coffee and studied day and night. After about a month of this he got so he couldn't concentrate and couldn't sleep. His professors said it was "burn out" and fairly common among academics. The University gave Jack permission to write his exams in the fall instead of the spring. Being a persistent person he worked during the summer getting into condition and preparing to write his exams. He prayed for help from God and kept meditating, affirming and chanting. With God's help he got his Bachelor of Commerce degree.

Later when he graduated from the University of Toronto with an MA in Industrial Psychology, Jack started his own business as a consultant. He was selling a new idea to management, telling them they could teach their managers how to hire and lead people. In spite of poor business results Jack kept praying, meditating and affirming and with God's help he was successful and developed three businesses that are profitable. Being a persistent person paid off handsomely.

One of Jack's hobbies is promoting the ideas and works of George Bernard Shaw. He attended the Shaw Seminar in Niagara-on-the-Lake for several years and was finally asked to speak on this program, which he did. This lead him to write a biography and a play on Shaw, which he submitted to the Artistic Director at Niagara-on-the-Lake. So far he has had no reply but being a persistent person he has retained an agent to try and get his works accepted. He is praying that God will help him to get his biography and play on Shaw published.

Chapter Three

ACTIVITIES

I think one of the best ways to appraise Jack is to examine the activities he has participated in and see how he has applied himself.

Business Executive: My boss is probably best known for his work in the field of business. It was a great struggle and took much persistence to develop three organizations which are profitable, because Jack selected the right people and gave them full authority and responsibility. He has a fourth company in the publishing business which we are struggling to develop into a profitable organization.

Jack however is not concerned about making profit in Creative Communication Consultants, as it is more of a hobby. He puts more effort into giving his books to people who need them than he does into making money. In spite of this there are great opportunities for this business to be very successful.

Speaker & Seminar Leader: The next activity that tells me something more about Jack is his speaking and seminar work. For more than twenty years he travelled constantly across Canada and the USA presenting programs to top and middle management. He was a pioneer in this field guiding the management of many organizations on how to hire and motivate people.

This activity revealed leadership ability, motivation and persistence.

He earned much of his living during his business career by making speeches or conducting seminars in the USA, Canada and England.

His public speaking took him all over Canada and the US. He was the only speaker to be invited back to the Sales Executive Club of San Francisco. He opened an office in New York in order to handle his speaking engagements in the US. Cruise companies contracted him to speak on their ships. He enjoyed this because he was allowed to bring his wife and friends.

At lunch Jack would speak humbly about his speaking engagements. It wasn't until one day I was reviewing some old files and I found a picture of him in front of what seemed 2,000 people. There he was on the podium; his arms were in an open gesture as if he was speaking to each person individually. The picture was literally worth a thousand words but Jack merely described these events as if they were little speeches he was doing to help managers.

Because of his love for public speaking, Jack took lessons from speech teachers to continually improve his delivery and he became very successful in this field. This skill enables him to present his ideas clearly in any setting. In the Rotary Club and the Arts and Letters Club he has become known as a leader and speaker in committees and meetings. Later in his career, he has spoken on spirituality to organizations.

Writer: Jack has written twelve books and although none of them have become best sellers in my opinion his books are excellent and very helpful to those who read them. I believe one day they will be best sellers.

Jack was inspired to write his book *Yes, You Can Quit Smoking* when reading that forty-five thousand people die in Canada each year from smoking. He was so shaken by this statistic that he dropped everything to write the book. I remember the lunch we had, where he announced that he must quickly get something publicized so that he could start to help save lives. This was yet another example of his generosity and spirituality. Many people have been able to give up smoking by reading this book and Jack continues to give it away to anyone who smokes or has friends or relatives who smoke.

The first book I worked on with Jack was *On the Path to Spiritual Fitness*. Jack has a vision to write several books on various aspects of spirituality. His idea is to make the book covers similar, so when people go to the stores they will be able to identify his books by their covers. The publishers have tried to sway Jack from his original vision but with little success. As I mentioned before, part of Jack's success is that he follows his beliefs until they are successful. Many people whom I have come to know through Jack, claim that *On the Path to Spiritual Fitness*, has changed their lives and given them faith in God.

In my opinion this book may some day become very popular and Godliness could become a well known religion.

As I mentioned previously, I can speak with first hand knowledge about *Improve Your Golf with Spirituality* because this book has helped me to improve my game.

Also Jack's latest book *Eustress: the Key to Success and Happiness* which is only in draft form, is already helping many people who have had the opportunity to read it.

All of these books have great potential for becoming popular and selling well when a marketing strategy is decided. Meanwhile, Jack continues giving books away to people who need them and want them.

Artist: Jack is much involved in the arts by his activities at the Shaw Festival. His biography and his play about Shaw have both been appraised by experts as very good but before he decides where to aim his effort on these manuscripts, he wants to hear from the Artistic Directors of the Shaw Festival because Jack would prefer to have his play about Shaw produced there rather than anywhere else.

Spiritualist: The writing of his book *On the Path to Spiritual Fitness* has revealed his activities in the spiritual field. Here Jack has demonstrated his qualifications to be called a spiritualist. He is constantly counselling people who read his books and as I previously mentioned he has made some speeches on spirituality.

Those who have read his books say they have given them a faith in God and changed their lives. Jack gives this book to those who show an interest in learning about God. This reveals his generosity and his giving attitude.

Student of George Bernard Shaw: One of his hobby activities is the study of George Bernard Shaw and his plays. Jack attended the Shaw seminars at Niagara on the Lake for more than ten years. Finally he was invited to speak on this program in 1986. Later he wrote a biography on Shaw and a play about him. I think this is an indication of his open mindedness and desire to learn plus his determination and persistence in trying to master everything he undertakes.

Golfer: Another activity is his hobby of golf. He was fortunate to join Rosedale Golf Club but lacked the skill to participate in the tournaments. When he describes the early days at Rosedale, he talks about how it was difficult for him to get playing partners because he didn't play very well. To improve his game Jack took lessons from the pros.

Fortunately Don Carrick, who had been Club Champion at Rosedale for many years and Canadian Amateur Champion in 1929 took an interest in helping him to play the game. This got Jack on the right path.

Carrick and Jack played for more than ten years, 3 or 4 times per week. Jack says that eventually Don let him win a game so Jack could boast about beating a former Canadian Amateur Champion. I don't believe it for a minute. I believe that Jack won fair and square because of his persistence, practice and dedication to the game. To be able to play to Carrick's standards revealed his athletic skill.

Over a period of many years, Jack took lessons from John Porter, the great pro at Rosedale. Much of his success in playing golf and writing his golf book have been due to the advice and training which Jack received from John Porter.

Rotarian: The Rotary Club of Toronto has always been a high interest of his because of the opportunity it gave him to help the underprivileged.

At Rotary he served on many committees and developed a Forum where he provided speakers that helped Rotarians keep up to date in ideas that would help them to work smarter for the underprivileged.

Jack conducted this Forum for ten years and it was one of his great disappointments that Rotary didn't adopt it as a permanent part of their program.

Army Officer: In 1942 Jack enlisted in the Canadian Army as a Lieutenant. Within a year he was posted to England where he helped to select officers. He speaks often of how his career in the Army taught him things that helped him in his business. This indicates his flexibility and leadership ability.

Family Man: Jack has been married twice. His first marriage broke up when he was overseas. In his second marriage he has five children and ten grand children and has been married to Audrey for fifty-eight years.

This indicates his ability to select the right person and to adjust to the ups and downs of marriage.

Club Man: Jack belongs to five prestigious clubs. He didn't seek membership in these clubs but was drawn into them by his friends.

He joined the Granite Club because a friend of his knew someone on the board of directors and urged him to join.

Another friend in the Sales and marketing Executives

Club offered to sponsor him at the Rosedale Golf Club. He didn't accept this offer but joined Rosedale at a later date when another friend Glen Wilton, offered to sponsor him.

Another friend Doug Kent took him to the Toronto Arts and Letters Club for lunch and as Jack admired the Club and its atmosphere of friendship and congeniality, Doug asked "Why don't you join?" and he did.

When playing golf his friend, Vlad Kavan, told him about his activities in the Royal Canadian Yacht Club. Jack expressed an interest in the club and the next Friday at Rotary Vlad had an application for Jack to join and had two members of the club standing by to second his application. This brought him a membership in another club.

Although he didn't seek out these memberships Jack enjoys his club activities as they have been an important part of his life both personal and in business.

Jack wanted to join the Rotary Club of Toronto. He wanted to join because the Club would give him opportunities to be of service. Eventually one of his corporate clients asked him to join and he was soon a member. For many years he was active serving on committees and participating in Rotary activities.

When in England during the war he automatically became a member of the Conservative Club in London because he was an officer in the Canadian army. It had overnight accommodation for members and Jack went to London every week end and stayed at the exclusive Conservative Club. He was hoping to meet Sir Winston Churchill who was also a member but this never happened.

Reader: Jack spends much time reading books. He gets many of his ideas from the latest non-fiction. He doesn't need to visit the library for ideas for his own books. He has his library at his home. When he hears or reads about a book that interest him, he buys it and puts it in his library.

Television Viewer: Jack has hundreds of channels on his television set and he spends about two hours each day watching TV. On the Discovery Channel, the Learning Channel, the History Channel and the Spiritual and Arts channels he gets many ideas for his books.

Financial Planner: Jack has saved some money and he spends considerable time reading about stocks and annuities and investing in the stock market. In the beginning he lost money. When he learned how to analyze stocks and when to buy and sell he has become reasonably successful as a trader in the stock market.

Chapter Four

PRAYING

To achieve his goals Jack has used certain methods which I will describe for you. In the next few chapters I have asked Jack to help me write his methodology for happiness, success and good health. You will read this advice and learn directly from the boss himself.

Jack believes that prayer enables you to have constant company, that you don't feel alone and that God is always with you. He believes that the most spiritual people feel the presence of God all the time. This is very therapeutic. When the chips are down and it comes to facing serious illness or death, you always feel as if you are on your own. Friends and relatives can be supportive, but they can't be with you all the time, but God is with you all the time. Praying makes you conscious of His presence. He is with you always because He is right in you. At your innermost center is God and your connection with Universal Power.

Jack feels that the most important thing in prayer is how you put your heart and soul into it by really concentrating. You must turn off the radio and television and try to find a completely quiet place where you are away from the sound of voices or any noise that would distract you. How you pray is a personal choice. Some people must kneel, others use the cross legged position while sitting on the floor. Others pray while they are walking, and others must pray out loud or in a church, temple or synagogue to feel that they are in contact with God. Jack feels you can use any of these methods or a combination of all. Pray whenever you can. Pray constantly. The more you pray, the more you will feel God's presence.

Jack has nearly always resorted to prayer when he has a problem or when he needs help with something. Fortunately in his prayers he has always been thankful and has shown appreciation for what God has done for him. In recent years this thankfulness has become a stronger part of his prayers and he has become grateful for all the advantages he has in life. He has also learned to be thankful for the distress in his life, which has taught him lessons and helped him to think clearly.

He has learned that it is also important to pray when things are going well. At these times you can give thanks and ask for guidance. By doing this you are kept constantly aware of God's presence. If you only pray when you need help or guidance, you tend to lose touch with God when things are going well. This is why many people are kept from the spiritual. They are enjoying life so much and have so much success that they keep thinking, "Who needs the spiritual?" So his advice is to pray constantly, no matter how you feel or what your situation in life. Keep in touch with God. He is the most important companion for you because He is with you all the time, even when you go to bed or go to sleep or when you leave this world.

With all the praying Jack has done in his life he believed that it was working. It just seemed natural to him to pray particularly when he needed help and guidance. He was never sure that prayer was working. He thought it was effective and he felt it was relieving distress but he had no proof that it was really bringing results.

Recently Jack read the book, *Healing Words*, by Dr. Larry Dossey, published by Harper Collins. He was convinced by the unquestionable evidence in the book that prayer does work. In many cases, described in Dr. Dossey's book under laboratory conditions, it has been proven that prayer does have the power to influence situations and make real changes and sometimes, dramatic changes.

Jack feels the best prayers are those which ask that, "Thy will be done". Praying that, "Thy will be done", is acknowledging that God knows what he is doing and the person praying should be adjusting to God's way of doing things. The person praying is asking God to empower him to have the strength to adjust to the world as God is running it. In other words, don't try to order the universe to run your way, but adjust to the way the Universe is running. If praying for some sick friend, for example, Jack could say, "Please God, let your spiritual energy flow through him and give him the strength to survive."

Here is an example of Jack's prayer program. If you are praying for several sick friends, your prayers will be more effective if you call them by name than if you just refer to them as your friends. Training in prayer is helpful. You will get better results as you practice more. Professional coaching from a minister, priest or rabbi could be helpful. As with anything new, seeking help to achieve your goal is a wise idea.

Use prayers of gratitude to show your appreciation of

what God has done for you. Here's a sample prayer that Jack uses.

> "Dear God, I am grateful for all the wonderful things you have given me. Thanks for my family, my home, my friends, my food, your love and understanding and the opportunity you have given me to live in a country where there is freedom of speech and freedom to change jobs and move somewhere else if I am so inclined."

Jack has learned that there are many things, which we are learning from research. For example, when faced with distress, you should pray constantly. When you are failing at something, call in God to help you. God wants to help, but he needs to be asked by prayers. God will always hear your prayers, so why not pray continually. In your prayers, ask anything according to His will, sometimes His will is different than yours.

Some pray according to what they want, instead of what God wants. Jack's belief is that you should devote your life to finding what God wants and, ask for the strength to follow his will. What God wants is for us to love ourselves, and others, to give service to others and to contribute something to the world. Do these things and pray for help in doing them, and God will help you.

As Jack learned more about praying he began to understand that praying for others is equally important. When people first turn to spirituality, they usually pray mostly for themselves. As they get further along the path to spiritual fitness, they start to pray more for others. God will answer your prayers for others, and at the same time, he will also answer their prayers for themselves. In order to help you, God must hear what you want and prayer is the way to ask him. There is nothing that God cannot do. No matter what distress you are facing he can help you to replace it with "Eustress", which is the stress you feel when something favorable happens to you.

God sometimes gives us a different and better result than we prayed for. The following prayer printed in *"Bits and Pieces,"* Economics Press, Fairfield N.J. a monthly booklet is one of Jack's favorite prayers and illustrates this point.

A Soldier's Prayer

I asked for strength that I might achieve.
I was made weak that I might learn humbly to obey.
I asked for help that I might do greater things.
I was given infirmity that I might do better things.
I asked for riches that I might be happy.
I was given poverty that I might be wise.
I asked for power that I might have the praise of men.
I was given weakness that
I might feel the need of God.
I asked for all things that I might enjoy life.
I was given life that I might enjoy all things.
I got nothing that I asked for, but everything
I had hoped for.
Almost despite myself my unspoken prayers were answered.
I am, among all men, most richly blessed.

Prayer may not work immediately because God is not always fast in answering prayers. He may be busy with other problems or He may not feel it is good for you to be relieved of distress right now. He may want you to do more thinking. Give God time to relieve you of the distress of what is bothering you. If you don't get relief in a few days, move on. Try Jack's meditation, which is your attempt to get God to communicate with you.

Chapter Five

MEDITATING

Jack has written many books on mental health and spirituality and he has found that meditation is an important way to get rid of distress and activate eustress. By meditating you can enter the alpha state, which is somewhere between being awake and asleep.

Jack sought the advice of meditation counsellors and therapists to help him learn how to meditate. The alpha state is the gateway to your spiritual life. It is the seat of the soul. It brings you access to your human potential. It brings you the knowledge that you are part of the Great Universe. It brings eustress into your life. Eustress is the stress you feel when something good happens to you.

Psychologists and philosophers have always said that we have a greater capacity and ability than we are using in our day-to-day life. We are all searching for the way to activate our minds so we can live to our fullest potential. Meditation can help you.

Many refuse to take meditation seriously. However, meditation can be quite dramatic in relieving distress and increasing eustress. Dr. Herbert Benson, M.D., in his book *The Relaxation Response*, suggests that there are four basic requirements to bring on the meditation feeling.

First you must have a quiet environment without distractions.

Second, you must have some object to dwell upon. This could be a word or a sound being repeated. The third requirement is a passive attitude. You should try to eliminate all thoughts and distractions from your mind. The fourth requirement is a comfortable position. For most of us the best position is probably sitting up straight in a comfortable chair and placing both feet squarely on the ground. Rest your arms on your legs, palms facing downwards. This is to allow the unimpeded flow of energy throughout your body. Don't lie down, or you may fall asleep. You can meditate lying down but it doesn't seem to be as effective for Jack as when he is sitting up. It may work for you.

To meditate effectively, you should close your eyes, and clear your mind, and try to have a positive attitude. Just allow thoughts to drift in and out of your mind and don't think about any problems in your life. Try to keep your mind blank and quiet.

Concentrate on your breathing. Allow a feeling of pleasantness and quietness to drift over you. You should have a syllable or word on which to focus. It could be any word. Jack suggests that "One" is a good word. Repeat the word over and over "One, One, One." Concentrate on your inhaling, breath coming and going. Continue repeating your word and maintaining a passive, peaceful attitude while concentrating on your breathing for 10 - 20 minutes twice a day. You can also do this anytime you feel distress. Ideally you should do it at the same time each day so you develop the habit. You can also do shorter periods of meditation during the day.

Sometimes you will find a meditation lasting five minutes very refreshing. It will bring eustress into your body.

During meditation, the sympathetic nervous system is not as active as during a waking moment. You may feel calm and at peace with yourself, or happy or ecstatically blissful. You should feel as if you are rising above the day-to-day routine, obligations and duties of life. Meditating twice a day should enable you to cope with life more effectively and bring eustress into your life. Jack meditates whenever he feels tension, just before a speech or an interview. It refreshes him and enables him to perform at his best.

For many years Jack used the type of meditation I have just described. He found this method of just closing his eyes and repeating a mantra to be effective. It helped him in many situations to relax. As he experimented with meditation he discovered a more effective method. What he now does is breathe in while he is counting to 4 and breathe out while counting to 4. The counting is his mantra. You could count to 3 in and out, or to 5, 6 or 7 in and out.

This type of meditation brings him relaxation. Jack helps it by trying to relax his arms and legs and all his body muscles. The result is a clearing of the mind and washing away of distress. He controls his mind by concentrating on his breathing. He keeps his mind on his stomach as he breathes in, and on his chest, as he breathes out.

Jack's suggestion for you is to experiment. Try different types of meditation until you find a method that gets you into the alpha state and keeps you there and brings you into contact with God. At first you may not get great results. Keep trying but don't push yourself. It should be a relaxing experience. I am giving you a formula that has worked for Jack. If you have any problems with meditation check with a professional. You will find experienced teachers at most Yoga training centers.

Meditation is a situation where God is usually talking to you instead of you talking to God, as you do in prayer. If you meditate once or twice a day, you may open the channel to the great Universal Power. This will give you a way to receive wise communications from the supernatural or from your unconscious mind. On a number of occasions while in this meditative state, Jack has received suggestions that have helped him to relieve distress. Meditation connects you with worldly life as well as spiritual life. It will bring you positive feelings.

In many types of meditation there will be times when you are bored and feel that you are achieving nothing. If you can persist, this boredom may pass and you will find your meditation more satisfying. One effect of meditation is to help you develop a new way of perceiving the world and relating to it. For most of those who have meditated it has brought them positive thoughts.

I am not trying to teach you how to meditate. I am telling you how Jack does it, hoping you will learn from him.

Although a meditative state will often come easy to some people, for others persistence and discipline are necessary. Often distress will interfere with your concentration. Keep trying to bring your mind back to your mantra and to your breathing.

Jack has found meditation very helpful when he is worried about something. If he has a problem that is causing him distress, meditation will usually give him the answer to the problem.

In the beginning meditation may cause you to be unhappy or distressed because it reveals to you a world with a different reality, which is a new way of perceiving things. Until you adjust to this newly conceived reality you may face some distress. Persist and you should eventually feel better.

As you meditate, various thoughts will keep coming into your mind. Jack just pretends these thoughts are in a parade on a float and lets them pass by. He recognizes them, but doesn't let them pull him away from his purpose of quieting his mind and activating eustress. The best way to control your thoughts is to concentrate on your stomach breathing in and your chest breathing out.

You can learn from reading, listening to sermons, educational programs and tapes. Meditation is another way of learning. By tapping into your inner strength, meditation gives you a new path to feeling good.

When your meditation period is over and you want to come back to your normal state, just count back audibly from five to one, visualizing the numbers in your mind and say out loud, "I am feeling better than before my meditation." You could also rub your hands together and rub your hands over your face as when you are washing. Try to come out of your meditation slowly and in a relaxed manner.

Jack looks forward to his periods of meditation, because it brings positive feelings to him. In meditation, he is hearing from God. In the first years of meditation, the biggest advantage to Jack was the ability to relax. But in the last few years with his new style of meditation, he feels that he is really in touch with God when he meditates. Meditation brings many benefits. Research is proving that it strengthens your immune system, improves your heart function and helps your heart to develop the right rhythm and brings you a positive attitude. However, the most important advantage to Jack is the communion with God.

Chapter Six

CHANTING

Another relaxing method Jack uses is chanting. If you can't feel good by meditating, try chanting.

Chanting has a powerful impact. Great symphony orchestras, violinists and pianists touch the soul when they play delightful music. Probably the most stimulating sounds come from military parade bands, which excite you, lift you up and activate your eustress. Jazz bands are equally stimulating in a different way. Romantic music can activate the passions and excite the loving instincts of those who dance or listen.

Sound and repetition are two very powerful stimulants. Chanting has them both. By chanting aloud and repeating your chant, you can bring eustress to your body. Some one once explained the repetition of chanting by saying, "*God isn't always listening. So you have to repeat.*"

Chanting bridges the gap between body and soul. By chanting prayers or affirmations you can rouse the spiritual feelings in yourself. It's sort of a combination of prayer and meditation. Spiritual masters chant to try and contact the divine. One saint described chanting as an ancient practise to join the worldly and the spiritual. Chanting helps to relieve distress.

Sounds of chanting enter the body through the skin and bones and stimulate the nervous system. It is well known that your tone of voice communicates as much as what you say. This reveals the power of sound.

Jack first became aware of the beneficial effects of sounds and music when he visited a sing-along bar in a small hotel. Everyone was singing with all their hearts and it made him want to sing. Each time he visited this sing along bar, he had eustress going for him. It was the sound, the repetition and the group effort.

When he started to write this piece on chanting, he felt that maybe he should skip it because he had little real experience with chanting. As he read more about it and thought about his experiences, he realized that he had been working with a form of chanting for nearly fifty years.

In his many management seminars, Jack had a technique for loosening up people and relaxing them, which was a form of chanting. Here's how it worked. Often on a Monday morning, he would have forty or fifty grim looking managers who were unhappy at the thought of taking a seminar. To get them in a better mood, he would ask them to stand up, hold their arms up in a 45 degree angle in front of them and look upward. Jack explains that they did this reluctantly, and then he would get them to follow him and jog around the room smiling and chanting.

"I am happy. I am happy. I am happy."

The results were like magic. The group now turned from a sullen quiet crowd to a joyful friendly gang. They were relaxed, laughing and talking to one another. The sound and the repetition and the moving around had really loosened them up. Although they resisted at first, they ended up enjoying the laughter and playfulness. This is a technique that other teachers in Jack's seminar business would learn to use.

At the time he didn't realize that this was a form of chanting and he used it successfully for many years on groups of up to 200.

How do you chant? Jack helped me to understand. Just say the words in a strong forced manner in a sharp tone with plenty of expression and fairly loud. Repetition is important. The words you use will have an impact and so will the repetition and the sound. You have three elements at work. I understand that most chanters sit down. Others stand. Jack's preference is to move around to try and get the body into the act. He likes to raise his hands up in front of himself to an angle of 45 degrees and look upward, smiling. Instead of standing still, he likes to jog around, which helps him to stimulate eustress.

Jack's favorite words for a chant are.

"I am happy, I am happy."

Other chants are,

"I am healthy. I am healthy." and "I am cheerful, joyful, happy, laughing."

You can also use your name for a chant. There is something magic in your name and chanting it increases your self-esteem. Your prayers and your affirmations also make good chanting material.

In order to make your chanting effective, focus on your words or phrases and put your heart and voice into it. Punctuate your chant with pauses and make it punchy. You should be presenting it in a voice that sounds like humming, singing and talking combined.

Chanting can be very helpful in activating good feelings. Keep using your prayers and spiritual affirmations when you chant.

For example, Jack will chant this prayer,

"Thank you God, I love you God, forgive me God, please help me God and help others. I am grateful God." and "I am positive, optimistic, enthusiastic and in excellent physical mental and spiritual health."

The reason for chanting is to change your mood from sadness to happiness and change your attitude from worldly thinking to spiritual thinking and eliminate distress.

Most of the great religions of the world have used chanting to help people become spiritually enlightened and connected with the Divine Presence. It is only recently that science has realized that chanting is good for physical, mental and spiritual health.

Fortunately chanting is not difficult to learn and each person can develop a technique, which fits his or her temperamental need.

Chanting is as important as prayer and meditation in helping a person to feel good. It gives us another path to God. I hope you will keep an open mind and try to learn to chant. It has been very helpful to me in developing spiritual fitness.

Chapter Seven

AFFIRMING

Another method for improving your attitudes is affirmating. Affirmations are positive thoughts on which you concentrate to achieve your goals. These thoughts can change your attitudes and alter your beliefs and get eustress working for you. Affirmations are really positive thoughts in vocal form. For example, Jack might try getting you to use this affirmation,

> "God is always within me, loving me, caring for me and guiding me. Thank you God, I love you God."

Jack is able to bring himself into the spiritual orbit and have the belief that God is always with him, by using affirmations.

Affirmations can reach into your subconscious mind to get it cooperating with you to activate eustress. The subconscious is powerful and has a great influence on your behavior and attitudes. It is important to get your subconscious working for you rather than against you.

Jack has explained to me that affirmations can assist you to bring success into your life. You can use affirmations to change your attitudes or to change your actions. You can create an affirmation to help you to eliminate distress and improve yourself. There are books, which will give you suggested affirmations. Two of these are, *Words that Heal*, by Douglas Block, Bantam Books, and, *What to Say When You Talk to Yourself*, by Shad Helmstetter, Pocket Books.

It is not difficult to create your own affirmations. Keep trying until you get an affirmation that feels just right. To create an affirmation, try this,

"God is always within me, loving me, caring for me and guiding me. Thank you God, I love you God."

It took Jack time and many repetitions until he felt it became just right. However, it may not be exactly right for you. Work at it until you find some wording that activates positive thinking for you.

There are a few things to consider about an affirmation if you want it to help you to relieve distress. First, it should be positive. Negative affirmations don't work. For example, if you are trying to reduce your weight, don't make an affirmation to get rid of a certain number of pounds. Rather make the affirmation positive. It could be,

"I am looking slim and healthy."

Second, you should always have your affirmations in the present. Don't make it,

"I am going to look slim and healthy,

but rather,

"I am looking slim and healthy."

An important factor to consider in using affirmations is that repetition helps. Keep saying it over and over during the day or when you are going to sleep at night or when you waken in the morning. Can you make it rhyme? Can you say it louder or with feeling? Can you chant it? Can you sing it? Can you visualize it happening when you repeat it? These techniques can be helpful in getting an affirmation that works. You can also make your affirmation more effective by including a thank you with it as Jack has done in this affirmation,

"God is always within me, loving me, caring for me and guiding me. Thank you God, I love you God."

Another way to strengthen your affirmation is to write it down. Make copies of it to put in prominent places such as, on your bedroom wall, or in your car. In this way, you will constantly visualize it. Jack believes there is an affirmation that will help you to relieve distress. It may take some work to find it. Keep experimenting. Make changes until you feel comfortable with your affirmation and until you feel it is working.

Jack helps me understand but also makes sure that I don't expect magic. Certain attitudes and ideas have been with all of us for a long time. If you have had a bad attitude about something for ten years maybe you should be satisfied to correct it in ten years with the right affirmation. Jack doesn't believe it will be this slow to work. If it isn't bringing you the results you want, try a completely new affirmation.

The best example Jack gives of how affirmations work is an experience he had. At one time he was very fearful, afraid of dying, afraid of getting sick, afraid of losing his energy and afraid of practically everything. A friend of his suggested that he had to get rid of these fears or they would cause him much distress. Jack agreed.

Because of these fears he made up an affirmation, which he repeated constantly in his meditation and chanting sessions. The affirmation was,

"I am brave, I am courageous, I am fearless because God is always within me."

He kept repeating this affirmation, morning, noon and night. Gradually, his fear disappeared and he became stronger.

This helped me when my son was injured in a motorcycle accident. He sustained several physical injuries and a brain injury. I called on Jack's examples of affirmation to see me through Robert's surgery and recovery. To this day as my son continues to recover I seek the advice and wisdom of Jack. His methods are simple and easy to use and practice has helped me stay focused on getting better and not to focus on the past.

The most powerful affirmations are short and to the point. Choose affirmations that seem right for you. Choose something in which you believe and which you feel you can bring into reality.

Jack says if you can bring God into your affirmation that will give it more strength. For example *"God is always helping me to be happy"* would be effective.

Chapter Eight

INTUITION

Jack also has strong feelings about intuition. He asks: "Do you believe in intuition? Do you ever get a hunch that you should do something or take certain action?" Something powerful is pulling you to make a purchase or to call someone on the phone that you haven't seen for a long time, or to check a certain file at the office. Often when I get this feeling and act on it, I find that it was the right thing to do. This is my intuition in action. Maybe your intuition enters somewhat into every decision you make.

The spiritual person knows that wise and understanding guidance is always available. It sometimes comes through impulses and hunches. These are messages from the spiritual world. The spiritual person respects suggestions that come through intuition and realizes that these ideas are coming from the great Universal Power and therefore pays close attention. This doesn't mean that the spiritual person follows every suggestion that comes through intuition but he investigates it. If a person doesn't understand an intuitive urge, they should ask God for help.

Jack tells me that intuition is knowledge that comes to you from spiritual sources which are beyond the five senses.

The spiritual part of intuition brings you information that doesn't always make sense in the real world. It may give you information regarding danger or risks you are taking or about which things are safe and which aren't. It is the Spiritual Power talking to you.

Here's an example of how intuition was brought to Jack's attention.

For sometime he had been suffering with a foot disability. He had tried several insoles and nothing seemed to be able to relieve his distress. This was on his mind one night when he went to bed. About 5 a.m. he was aroused from his sleep by a sudden urge to get up and turn on his television. He rejected this urge because he never watched T.V. in the middle of the night and he was tired.

Intuition or wisdom kept urging him to turn on his T.V., which he finally did. There to his amazement was an advertising program about a pair of insoles, which seemed just what he needed to relieve his foot distress.

Jack is a believer. Information that comes to him from his intuition may be as important as food and drink. So pay attention to your intuition. Check it out. Sometimes it knows more than you do, but be cautious. If it makes sense when you get the facts about the alternative choices you have in each situation, you can take some action.

Paying attention to your intuition should help you to get positive things going so you can lead a more productive life.

Chapter Nine

WIDENING YOUR INTERESTS

Another thing that I have learned from Jack is that in order to achieve the goals you want you should fill your life with activities at which you can win, achieve, learn, develop your skills, create, meet new people, travel, and help people with their problems.

This belief in wide interests will also enable you to relax. When you are tired you don't always need a rest, you may need a change of pace. Often you hear the saying "A change is as good as a rest". Jack believes that wisdom comes partly from wide interests that bring you into contact with many people and many different situations from which you learn. Wide interests also help you to get along better with others.

Who do you like best, a person who is sitting at home staring into space or one who is active and doing interesting things? Personally I find the actve person, more interesting. Jack also points out that another advantage of wide interests is that you become more creative. Usually creative ideas come from one of your activities. Those with wider interests have more experiences from which to draw creative ideas.

It is also known that wider interests improve your mental health. Jack has done much research on this. The more activities in which you participate the more sources of satisfaction you have and the more emotional support you have in adjusting to the adversities of life.

If you eliminate one activity, you still have several other satisfying ways to spend your time. I found this out when my son became ill and I had to eliminate several activities in order to take care of him. But because I had several interests, I was left with something to keep me mentally fit.

One stimulating activity is the work I do with Jack. Having lunch with him each week is also pleasant. Jack tells us that each successful activity in which you invest your time brings you satisfaction, which gives you enthusiasm for your other activities.

Abraham Maslow, the father of Humanistic Psychology has said that to be happy and healthy we must each do everything we are capable of doing. In other words, to lead a full life and be great, we must be able to use all of our talents. Life is a struggle to find our talents and use them to the fullest.

Jack explained to me that the development of good mental health begins at childhood. Babies are not born neurotic; babies don't worry. They learn how to worry as they grow up. When a child is born he is completely dependent on his parents to feed him, clothe him and keep him doing interesting things. As he matures, he struggles to become independent. He does this by substituting dependence on activities in his life and on other people, for dependence on his parents. As time goes by he gains the contacts and skills necessary to stay in a good state without depending on his parents.

First he gets to associate with and depend on his own friends at school. He soon gets interested in academic subjects. Then he gets active in sports.

This draws him away from his parents some more. Next he develops a hobby, perhaps collecting stamps. Eventually he discovers a philosophy of life and starts to believe in something bigger than himself. Then he gets a job in which he becomes absorbed. Finally he falls in love and creates a family of his own, which puts him in the best state of all and frees him from dependence on his parents.

The person who fails to develop adequate supports to replace his parents is in danger of falling into a weak state, and he may also drive his parents to the psychiatrist. The truth is that nobody is capable of being completely independent. We all need supports to keep us in a good state.

To help you find the right kinds of activities that will bring you satisfaction, Jack suggests that you go back in your life history and try to recall anything you did at any time of your life which you enjoyed doing, did well and felt good about. Don't concern yourself about the situation in which you did these things. It could have been as a hobby or in your academic or sports life or at your work. As long as you enjoyed it, did it well and felt good about it, start doing it again. Things you like doing are like diamonds in the rough. Pounce on them and keep doing them.

Undoubtedly you can recall a time when you were feeling depressed. You were invited to a party but the last thing you wanted to do was go. You forced yourself to go, and later you found you were quite exhilarated by the contacts with others, the stimulating interchange of ideas, and the challenge of making new friends. This put you in a great state. Your depression was reduced by the time you got home. People contacts have a positive effect on your state; the person who is socially active is more likely to feel good and enjoy life than a person who keeps to himself. Successful contacts with people are very important to your mental health.

This always works for Jack. He suggests that if you are worried about something, plunge headlong into your favorite hobby of woodworking, stamp collecting, bricklaying, scuba diving, golf, or mountain climbing. Jack likes to exercise; it allows him to focus on something mundane but a bit strenuous. It also helps the endorphins get working to make him feel better medically. After a few hours of participation in the activity he most enjoys, he will feel more relaxed and in a better state. He may even find that his problem has been resolved by his subconscious mind.

Jack believes that a hobby should be something you enjoy doing. It must not be a chore. It should be an escape from day to day routine, an activity in which you can totally lose yourself. If this type of activity gives you satisfaction from achievement, this will change your mood and give you good feelings. It doesn't matter what your hobby is, as long as you find it interesting, absorbing and rewarding. Anything at which you can achieve, learn, create, develop a skill, meet new people or help people with their problems will put you in a state that will make you feel good and stimulate you to take action, to solve your problems.

Sports are ideal as a hobby. Sports offer an outlet for tension and excess energy and also contribute to body conditioning. Game sports in particular provide a challenge because of the competition involved. The "team spirit" alone may change your state and give you energy. Playing the game well also brings you satisfaction, which helps to move you into a better state.

The body thrives on physical challenge and the mind thrives on mental challenge. For this reason Jack believes that every person should have some physical and mental interests in their life, something that goes beyond selecting the right necktie. Jack suggests that you pick some field like mathematics, history, psychology, philosophy, anthropology, geography, astronomy and start to do some studying. It doesn't cost money either, you can get books from the library or from the internet.

If you can afford to, take a night-school course at your local university, this not only will develop your mind and put you in a new state, but it will also widen your interests and thereby help to make you wiser and more creative. It will also put you in a new situation where you can meet people that are also looking for the same thing as you.

George Bernard Shaw said that he found thinking so stimulating that it was more pleasurable than sex. This indicates what powerful satisfaction thinking can bring to you and what an exalted state it can put you in. Jack's advice is to get some kind of physical and mental challenge going for you so you will have several ways to get yourself into a positive state.

Chapter Ten

LAUGHING

Jack suggests that you go back over your life and find all the things that have made you feel good. Put these things on a list and keep constantly visualizing them. Whenever you are not feeling well, go over these things in your mind and keep visualizing them. This exercise will give you a way to avoid falling into a depressed state. Jack believes in the importance of laughing and this is a big part of what makes him successful. The saying, "laugh and the world laughs with you" is so true. He laughs as much as he can. Jack has helped many people bring laughter into their lives.

Here is a simple technique Jack shares on how you can get yourself to laugh right now. It's easy! Just create an artificial laugh. Just chant "ha ha ha – ha ha ha – ha ha ha" and your state will begin to change. Keep up this artificial laugh and smile while you are doing it. Stand straight and look up. Keep moving around and visualize yourself being happy and joyful and you should soon improve your state. If you do it right, you can add joyous happy feelings to your artificial laugh. It works.

I like this one the best. Jack tells people to think of one of the funniest incidents you can remember. Try to get the feeling of that humorous situation. Visualize yourself right back in that incident and in a great humorous state. Think of what you saw and heard and how you felt on that occasion. How were you standing or sitting? Make the mental picture brighter, clearer more colorful, larger and move it in close to yourself. Reproduce your posture and what you saw, heard and felt. Now at the height of your humorous feeling take a deep breath and go "ha ha ha – ha ha ha – ha ha ha" and at the same time press your thumbs against your forefingers.

Linger mentally in this humorous situation and do your artificial laugh several times with your thumbs and forefingers pressing together. You should now be anchored to this joyous situation and you should be able to bring this feeling back anytime by visualizing it and going "ha ha ha – ha ha –ha – ha ha ha" and pressing your thumbs and forefingers together. Try it. Jack advises that if it doesn't work the first time, keep trying.

Here is another technique that Jack uses. Anchor yourself to other happy, fun situations in the same way. Go back in your imagination and get the exact feeling of fun you had in another situation. What did you see, hear and feel, how were you sitting and standing. Turn up the brightness on this mental picture, make it colorful, large, clearly focused and move it close to yourself. Try to reproduce it exactly as you experienced it. Now at the height of the fun when the punch line has been told, take a deep breath and repeat "ha ha ha – ha ha ha – ha ha ha" and press your thumbs and forefingers together on each hand. Hold this feeling for a while and repeat the exercise several times. Now you have anchored yourself to another fun situation that will bring back a joyful feeling anytime you want it.

Have you ever been in a depressed mood and then somebody made a humorous comment or a funny joke and suddenly you broke into laughing and into a new state of mind and body? It happened immediately. Or have you ever been in a solemn group where there is some conflict and it looks as if things are turning into a fighting situation and someone suddenly makes a humorous comment and in a flash everyone starts to laugh and immediately all are in a great state?

Laughing is one of the fastest ways to put yourself and others into a favorable state. So here I have given you Jack's method of using laughter to change states quickly. Jack also wants you to look into the possibility of using humour in your life to constantly help keep you in a positive state.

Comedians earn fabulous incomes because they can take a group of tired, worried business men or women and suddenly change their mental states and get them smiling and laughing.

People with a sense of humour who can bring fun and laughter into almost any situation are the most popular people because we all want to improve our states of mind and we welcome anyone who can help us do it. Men who have the most success with women are those who can make them laugh. When a woman starts to laugh she changes state, feels good and looks favorably on the man who can do it.

In the human relations area, laughter is one of the best techniques for getting along with people of both sexes and gaining their support. A woman with a sense of humour is desirable to a man because when she gets him laughing she puts him in a state to enjoy her company.

In the public speaking profession, the best communicators are those who mix their serious comments with funny lines. People like to laugh because it makes them feel good. They like to be entertained while they are learning. The highest paid speakers are humorists as well as educators.

Jacks asks "How much do you laugh? Are you enjoying life? How much pleasure are you getting out of life?" These are the first questions he would ask you to determine your mental health.

How much you laugh will tell if all is well. It will tell if you are liking life and feeling good. These are the clues that indicate you are enjoying life. If you are unhappy and worried about something and are suffering with distress you can change this if you can laugh.

Because the main symptom of mental ill health is unhappiness, worry and depression, it seems to Jack that the front line of attack against mental ill health should be to try and keep happy. He puts it this way; when you start to over-worry and get depressed, this is a signal that something is wrong. You are either doing something that is unhealthy or you are thinking in a way that puts you in a bad state.

Nothing is more important than laughter in your growth and development. When you are laughing, it's nature's signal that you are in a good state, making progress. Laughter brings you very positive feelings. It gives you strength to do all the things you must do for success. It makes you more confident and helps you to think well of yourself. It enables you to appreciate life and all its blessings. It keeps you in a good state.

Jack urges you to get pleasure from achieving, learning, creating, developing your skills, travelling, meeting new people, and helping people with their problems. Doing these things will bring on good feelings Relaxing, meditating, laughing, philosophizing and day-dreaming can also bring you happiness. These inner pleasures can be just as great as the pleasures that come from activities.

Many people who are striving to be rich and famous are unhappy because they are always looking forward to the day when they will have more money or be prime minister or president. There is nothing wrong with being ambitious, but there are many things wrong with passing up present joy and pleasure for an uncertain future.

In our day-to-day struggle to survive and make a living, we have tended to become too serious. The grim pursuit of work and the difficulties of getting the job done have absorbed many of us so much that we have put laughter, pleasure, having fun and enjoying life on the back burner. The pursuit of achievement, power, skill, money and status has taken over and we are in a more serious state than nature intended.

The original man in the jungle was a playful, fun loving person who had to struggle to eat and survive but his capacity to play and laugh and enjoy life and keep in a relaxed state gave him relief from distress, fear and insecurity. He didn't return home to his cave with ulcers because other cavemen had collected more bananas than he. Playing and laughing were a very important part of life in the jungle.

Mentally healthy people are in a happy state. Mentally sick people are generally in an unhappy and depressed state. So if you want to keep mentally healthy, Jack advises get some fun into your life. Relax and play more and enjoy life and laugh as much as possible. This will put you in a positive state. If you can do this you will get along better with people and be more effective at your work.

Action always comes first. If you want to be confident, act confident and you will eventually be confident. If you want to be happy, act happy. If you want to enjoy life, act as if you are enjoying it. So sing, whistle, and laugh whenever you can. Keep using your artificial laugh "ha ha ha – ha ha ha – ha ha ha" and press your thumbs and forefingers together.

There is much evidence that fun, humour and laughter affect not only our mental health but our physical health. Throughout history, the great thinkers and philosophers have been telling us that humour and laughter are therapeutic. Freud said that humour was a good way to counteract nervous tension. Emmanuel Kant said that laughter produces a feeling of good health and stimulates the body processes.

Jack describes a good example of how effective laughter can be in the health area. Norman Cousins, author of *Anatomy of an Illness* (Bantam Books) helped cure himself of an apparently incurable physical disease by thinking positively and laughing as much as possible.

Norman Cousins had been advised by his doctors that he had a crippling disease that was incurable and that his chances of survival were very slight. He decided to abandon traditional medical treatment and to treat himself by stimulating his positive feelings. He decided to try and think positively and laugh as much as possible.

He arranged to get amusing presentations such as reruns of the old television show "Candid Camera" and some old Marx Brothers' movies. He soon found that ten minutes of laughter had a positive effect on his physical condition. He kept watching humorous films and also had his nurses read him humorous books to try and keep him laughing.

The treatment worked and he started to become healthier. He proved scientifically that his laughing treatment was working by taking blood sedimentation readings before and after each session of laughing. Each time he did this there was a drop of about five points. This trend stayed with him and provided him a gradual improvement. He was excited to discover that there was a physiological basis for the theory that laughter is good for you.

Norman Cousins was learning about the tremendous capacity of the human mind and body to recover, even under very adverse conditions, and that there is a natural drive in the human mind and body toward good health.

Appreciating and protecting this drive is important to us all. The way to do it, according to Jack, is to keep laughing as much as possible.

Unfortunately, humour that triggers laughter is very difficult to generate. We continue to tell the same old jokes with variations, and comedians steal jokes and funny situations from one another, because to produce humour is a very difficult task. Will Rogers, Stephen Leacock, Woody Allen, James Thurber, Mark Twain, Dorothy Parker, Groucho Marx and a few other writers and performer have been able to create original humour and we revere them for this rare talent. Bob Hope, George Burns, Bill Cosby, Eddie Murphy, Red Skelton, Johnny Carson and other comedians have become rich because our society is willing to pay a big price in order to laugh.

Jack alerts us to benefits that can come to us from laughing. Physiologically, laughing stimulates your blood circulation and exercises your lungs. It also exercises your diaphragm, which is a muscle between your chest and your stomach. If you put your hand on your stomach while you are laughing, you will feel the diaphragm moving up and down, exercising the muscles in this area of your body.

When you laugh, it causes you to breathe more deeply and take more oxygen into your blood. The entire heart-lung-blood delivery system benefits when you laugh. Laughter is very relaxing to your body as well as to your mind and emotions. When you laugh at something, you forget your problems, at least temporarily.

The experts tell us that laughter produces endorphins in the brain which reduce pain. When you laugh you get a new slant on life because you become less intense, more objective and not so deeply involved.

The desire to feel good and be happy is one of the greatest needs of human beings.

Some great thinkers have said that the purpose of life is to feel good. Feeling good is an indication that your life is going well and you are in a good state. Having pleasure and enjoying life and laughing may be the secrets of success. This is why successful people tend to be fun-loving people. When I first discovered this, I thought that these people were happy because they were successful. But I later found that they were more likely to be successful because they were happy.

Some writers have declared laughter to be beneficial because it restores homeostasis, stabilizing blood pressure, oxygenating the blood, massaging the vital organs, stimulating circulation, facilitating digestion, relaxing the system and producing a feeling of well-being.

In spite of the physical changes that take place when you laugh, Jack is sure that the psychological and emotional changes are just as important.

The playful attitude that encompasses you and the resulting relaxation are the most therapeutic actions you can take to make you feel good. You can't be suffering from distress when you are laughing. Try to worry and laugh at the same time. It's impossible!

To Jack this means that we should take action in our lives, which will bring us pleasure and cause us to smile or laugh. If successful mentally healthy people, are happy people who enjoy fun and laughing, one of the best routes to success and happiness is to search for all the things in your life that you like to do, that you do well and that make you feel good. Spend as much time as you can doing these things, so you will enjoy life and laugh as much as possible.

Laughter is something spontaneous that comes upon us when we see or hear something that we think is funny. Psychologists have tried to discover what make us laugh. Their findings indicate that it is something that changes our train of thought suddenly. If your mind is following a certain line of reasoning and suddenly it is changed, then the surprise of the change will make you laugh.

Jack experimented with his granddaughter when she was two years old. When playing peek-a-boo, she looked quite puzzled as he stuck his head around a wall and said, "Peek-a-boo." If he got down on his knees and peeked at her from a completely different position, she smiled and broke out laughing. Each time he fooled her and appeared in an unexpected place, it was funny to her.

Humour can also come from exaggeration. For example, Jack once said that he had no enemies. He had outlived them all. This was an exaggeration, of course, but funny because it was unexpected. The same could be achieved with an understatement. Groucho Marx at one time was considering suing a certain publication for slandering him. His lawyers were planning to take the case to court but Groucho said first he would write to the publishers and see if he could get them to be reasonable. So he wrote that unless they published a retraction of the article about him he would cancel his subscription to their magazine. This was an unexpected reply and an understatement. The unexpected can also come about by suddenly changing a train of thought. For example, "You can keep young by dieting and exercising and by lying about your age!" This last comment is unexpected because it changes a train of thought.

Another way to get a laugh is with the humorous catalogue. This is a situation where you have a list of items to which you add an item at the end of the list that is unexpected and out of context. For example, Jack might say that he is a great golfer because he has a smooth swing, putts accurately, chips and pitches with precision, and he can't add! The last item is out of context and unexpected and will get a smile or a snicker or a belly laugh depending on to whom you are telling it.

Jack advises us to keep watching for situations where we can exaggerate, understate, suddenly change our train of thought or create a humourous catalogue and you should be able to create more humour as you go about your daily rounds. Of course there are other ways but these are the best. Create humour to amuse yourself and to get eustress going for you. Don't expect many brilliantly funny lines. Creating humour is very difficult. If you can do it easily and effortlessly, you may become happy and rich!

Chapter Eleven

TAKING ACTION

Having an open mind and being willing to try new things is very important if you want to be successful. New ideas may bring suggestions that will help you in many ways. Taking action is also important if you want to become successful. Sitting back and waiting for things to happen is not what Jack is all about.

Many people are afraid to try new things. Jack has learned that by experimenting and taking control of his actions leads him down new paths. Much of his participation in reflexology, shiatsu, massage, acupuncture, homeopathic medicine and naturopathic medicine have all been methods that have helped him and the contacts with these professionals have been therapeutic.

The people who have administrated these techniques have all been supportive of Jack with their counselling and guidance. He has become friends with most and he looks forward to his treatment sessions.

Jack has received much strength from the things in his life which have made him feel good. He urges his clients to review their life's history and search for anything that has brought them happiness or success. Write down all of these things and keep visualizing them. Whenever you feel discouraged or depressed, think about these things and keep visualizing them.

Keeping these favourable things in mind will be stimulating and should make you feel good when you renew them. This action gives a person support in times of adversity.

Another activity which Jack recommends is contact with people. He takes action when it comes to meeting with people. Jack will dive right in and try to draw people out of their shell. He does this in groups or with individuals.

As Dr. Dean Ornish has discovered in his research, meeting with people is as important to your health as giving up smoking, exercising, dieting or inherited qualities. He has spelled this all out in his book *Love and Survival*.

Here is an example of Jack taking action. When he left the army he decided to return to university and become a psychologist. Unfortunately he had never taken any undergraduate psychology so he didn't have the qualifications to get into the graduate psychology program.

However, he did persist in applying for this course.

Eventually the head of the department said that the only way he could get Jack into graduate psychology, would be to have him take the required undergraduate psychology courses while he was studying for his MA.

Although this would be a big load to carry Jack agreed to try it. Fortunately he loved psychology and didn't mind the work involved but the amount of study and writing required was stressful. By working hard Jack was able to qualify on both his undergraduate and graduate studies and by persisting he became a psychologist.

Being a psychologist turned out to be only one of his careers. By continually challenging himself and taking action, Jack ended up with two University degrees, was a consultant in psychology, conducted many seminars all over America and has started three businesses

Jack has written 12 books on business, health and spirituality. He has his own library with over 200 books. Whenever he hears of a new book on health, business or spirituality he buys it and adds it to his library.

On the personal side his accomplishments are no less. He has been married 58 years, has 5 children of whom he is very proud and ten grandchildren.

He belongs to 5 clubs. If you ask Jack about his clubs he will tell you that they have been instrumental in helping him in business, however I also believe that the clubs and the way he supports them, help keep him up to date. These activities continually give him ways of staying current with not only the business world, but the world of politics and the arts.

Jack also plays golf fairly well. Just recently he was golfing with one of his sons, his granddaughter and a friend. Jack was a little late for the golf appointment, so when he arrived in a bit of a hurry, everyone had teed off. He stepped up to the tee box, placed his ball and drove it 175 yards straight down the fairway. Everyone was impressed and they continued to play. Unfortunately the weather became quite cold, so he and his granddaughter made their way home after six holes.

This situation gave him great satisfaction and he put it on a list of things that he thinks about when he wants to feel good.

He continues to amaze all who know him.

Chapter Twelve

EXERCISING

Jack constantly reminds me that one's physical behavior has a powerful influence on your mental state. You will notice that when you have the flu or a bad cold, you get depressed. On the other hand, whenever you jog or swim or play a game of tennis or golf or do anything physically active, you immediately begin to feel better. As I mentioned before, getting those endorphins working not only helps you mentally but the physical activity helps your circulation, gets more oxygen into your system, pushes more blood into your brain, and clears out the clouds of doubt and worry.

All your behavior is the result of the thinking and visualizing you do. When you feel strong and resourceful, you will do things you otherwise wouldn't. If you feel you can't do something, try changing your physical stance. Act as if you can do it. If you stand straight, look up, breathe deeply, smile and act as if you can do it, you probably will. To do your best you must stand and act as powerfully as possible. This always amazes me but it works. I have trained myself to follow this method of making sure I stand straight and walk confidently, even when I feel like withering. People always comment on how much confidence I exude. I have often been asked if I am an owner of a business, because of the way I have trained myself to walk and act confidently.

Another method Jack has taught me is if I want to motivate myself to do something, think back to a time when I did it before and remember it clearly. I get right back into the situation in my imagination and remember how I was standing or sitting or moving and how I was looking. I reproduce my physiology exactly as it was. When I do this, I have the same motivational urge that I did when I did it the first time.

There's no super action without the physical backup. Physiology is a powerful tool. It works fast and consistently. If you change your posture, breathe deeply, relax your muscles, smile, look up and move around briskly, you will change your state.

Jack says that depression is a mental state, but it can be brought on by physical behavior. If you walk around with your eyes down, your shoulders bent forward, a worried look on your face, take shallow breaths, and talk to yourself in a sad monotone, you will experience distress. A depressed body gives signals to the mind to start worrying. If somebody tells you he is depressed, ask him how he does that. He has to be doing something physical and mental to get himself into a depressed state. If he changes his physiology and focuses on the positive and makes pictures in his mind of him achieving exciting goals, he will likely snap out of it.

The right changes in your body can change your state. Elvis Presley's success was due greatly to the fact that he expressed his feelings physically, which put him in a powerful mental state. By a combination of physical, vocal and feeling actions, he could put an entire audience into a great state.

Rock stars and bandleaders put a lot of body into their act. How about cheer leaders? They have physical actions that signal their brains to be positive. By chanting and moving, they bring a lot of emotion into their act and move people by their visual, auditory and feeling senses. Ballet dancers, gymnasts, figure skaters, tennis players, golfers, runners and jumpers become dynamic performers when they get moving. Physical action changes their state and gives them the power to do what they are trying to do.

To help get the most powerful message to his brain, Jack copies the physical moves of great performers whom he admires. He lets his body help move his brain into the most powerful state. Then he is able to do anything for which he has the talent. You will notice that I am not telling you how to exercise but I am telling you how Jack exercises. If you plan to do any of these exercises, check with your doctor first.

To tap more of his inner power, Jack starts copying the physical behavior of people who are very successful. When he does this, he finds his brain working in a new way. He copies their gestures, stance, and facial expressions. He soon notices a difference in his feelings and behavior. There is no faster, more dynamic way to achieve what others are doing than through physiology.

According to Jack, people who succeed are those who combine their mental and physical powers to achieve their goals. Coordination of mental, spiritual and physical effort is the secret of strength. When your body, your words and your mental pictures are coordinated, you are giving signals to the brain and it delivers the results you want. If you say to yourself,

"I can do that", and your breathing, posture and facial expressions are right and you can visualize yourself doing it, you can accomplish it.

It's not difficult to move into a state that brings you eustress but to keep in this state is another story. This requires keeping constantly fit. The first step toward getting into a good permanent physical condition is to get rid of any excess weight so you can move around easily and so your body won't have the strain of carrying around extra pounds. Let's see what you can do to rid yourself of excess weight and help you keep in a more joyous state.

To begin with, Jack suggests you make a list of all the reasons why you want to lose weight. Like everything else you do, knowing the "why" behind it is a great motivator. Here are some of the "whys": Being over-weight will interfere with your health. Every extra pound you carry around is an extra burden for your heart. It contributes to high blood pressure, diabetes, strokes, heart attacks and probably cancer.

The positive "whys" are to enable you to move around more smoothly and generally look better. Being slim brings out the best in your appearance but it will also enable you to be more successful in sports, dancing, walking and other physical activities. You will feel better about yourself. You will know that you are doing your best to keep healthy and to look your finest. It will bring you joy and peace of mind to know that you are not carrying around excess weight. That interferes with everything you do.

Jack loses weight by exercising and eating less food. He gets all the exercise he can get. He walks to work, he walks everywhere possible. If he must take his car, he parks it a distance from his destination and walks the balance of his trip.

In the next chapter Jack will show you how he plans a healthy diet so he can keep his weight down.

Chapter Thirteen

DIETING

Follow the program Jack recommends and you will put yourself in control of your eating habits. You will be like the captain of a ship who knows exactly what port he is heading for and where all the dangerous waters are. You will steer yourself directly to slimness knowing that you can lose pounds by eating less. You can start right now and get some results immediately. Are you ready for the challenge?

Jack doesn't tell you what to eat but he tells you what he eats to keep feeling good.

Jack's diet is made of 70% water content foods such as fruits and vegetables. He is always interested in following his progress on a chart and gets a thrill out of guiding his graph exactly where he wants it to go until he has reached the exact weight he desires. He is in control every bit of the way. It also gives him a sense of power to see that he can bring his weight down. As you watch him decide on what foods he wants, you will be deciding what you want. Be sure and check with your doctor before making any changes in your diet.

Dieting is an educational process. You are learning about yourself, about foods, and about living when you start to be more selective in your eating habits. Dieting is a challenge, but you have the guts to win. Follow your plan. Get rid of that excess weight and feel good.

Jack advised you to find out just how much food you must eat each day to keep your weight down and carry out your normal activities. Eat only enough to give you energy, build your body, and keep your sex life going at top speed. It may take some time to establish how much food you really need, and you will be amazed to discover how small this amount actually is. When you eat less, you will get more pleasure from the food you eat. You may be eating a great buffet every day when what you need is more fruits and vegetables.

Eat your meals slowly. Don't plan to have a six course meal during a television commercial. Chew your food well: don't gulp it down. This will help your digestive system to cope with food more easily.

Jack advised if you haven't lost some weight by the end of your first week, eat less next week. If your weight is still not down, don't be discouraged. At the beginning of any diet it is usually difficult to get results and you may even gain some weight. Keep working at it and keep weighing yourself every day.

Jack suggests that next week you drop from your taboo list some items that you are accustomed to eating each week and extend your exercising by a little more time and you will be on target at the end of two weeks with some weight loss.

Remember the six course dinner is the sort of activity that leads to over weight. So keep your meals simple. Include only two or three kinds of foods that are easy to digest and less likely to result in overeating. By mixing varieties of foods, you stimulate your appetite and tend to eat more than you would if only two or three kinds of food were available.

According to Jack your appetite is a very poor guide to the amount of food you really need. Sometimes you can get up from an extremely heavy meal and five minutes later you are ready to start all over again. This tremendous appetite is a carry-over from the days of early man. His appetite developed so that when he found food he would gorge himself, thus storing energy for possible famine days ahead. Since we are not likely to experience famine in our modern western civilizations, try to stop eating while you're still hungry.

Jack says keep food out of sight. Don't leave chocolates, cake, candy, cookies or peanuts lying around the house. If your kitchen and dining room look like the windows of a delicatessen, you're in trouble. Out of sight, out of mind does apply to food. Your willpower is bound to waver if it is constantly being nudged by a luscious chocolate cake sitting on the kitchen shelf. You will nibble for the same reason people climb Mount Everest - just because it is there.

When you are shopping, buy only foods that are good for you. Resist the temptation to drop several packages of potato chips into the shopping cart.

Don't buy foods that are fattening, so you won't have them around the house to tempt you. And be sure not to shop on an empty stomach, when you are most likely to grab for junk foods.

Those innocent little tidbits you keep sneaking do add up. Two cookies are 100 calories. If you eat two cookies or the equivalent every day for 35 days, you add a pound of weight to your frame. In a year this adds 10 pounds.

Jack asks "Who needs it?" Instead, have some fresh fruit and vegetables at all times in your refrigerator, and when you get really hungry help yourself. These are the things that give you the vitamins and minerals you need, keep your graph on target and keep you in control. Remember, weight doesn't usually come from gorging but from constant munching.

You can still enjoy dinner parties and dining at fine restaurants. Substitute clear soup for cream soup and vegetable juices for pâté. Order lean meat with a baked potato and lightly cooked vegetables or salad. Skip the heavy salad dressing and skip dessert. No one needs to know you are being selective about your food unless you stand on your chair, beat your chest and scream because you can't have dessert.

According to Jack anger or boredom and worry may often cause you to turn to food for relief. That is why you should engage in some physical activity instead of eating. Run, skip, hit a golf ball, or bounce a basketball. Get into the habit of exercising when you find yourself in a negative mood. Contrary to popular opinion, exercising will lower your urge to eat. So keep moving as much as you can all day long.

So you don't grieve over the loss of certain foods, keep yourself occupied. Keep busy with work, hobbies, and social activities. If you are busy and active you will forget about eating. The less active you are and the more time you have on your hands, the more your thoughts will turn to food. Sitting alone in your room will only cause your mind to drift to fantasies of roast beef, chocolate fudge cake and banana splits. Or you may see yourself running on a beach covered with chocolate chip cookies. The life of leisure is a sure road to obesity.

Late night snacks can be really damaging because your body doesn't have a chance to burn them off. Jack advises you try to keep so busy that you go to bed tired; too tired to eat.

Jack advises that when you are hungry between meals, start to think of the goals you have set for yourself. Close your eyes and see yourself as a slim, energetic person with your graph carrying you to your goal. Then go and take some action on your latest hobby; whether it is perfecting your tennis stroke, mastering the violin or cultivating cucumbers.

Jack will tell you never lose more than a pound a week. By losing weight slowly, you will have the chance to adjust to the new you and you will avoid the shock that will come from suddenly losing too much weight. You will also slowly change your eating habits so your weight loss will be permanent. Do it this way and you will know that you are doing the sensible thing. Be sure to get the approval of your doctor.

If you do it right, dieting can be fun. Nothing is more important to you than the food you eat. It is a fascinating game to see how different foods increase or decrease your weight and energy. It will also be fascinating to fit smoothly into your dress or pants.

Remember I am not recommending what foods you should eat. I am not a dietician. I will only tell you what Jack is eating and you can decide on your own diet with the approval of your doctor.

Chapter Fourteen

LOVING

You can pick up almost any self-help book today and you will get advice that you can cure all your human relations problems and relieve yourself of distress by loving others. To Jack it seems maudlin to go around loving everyone. Especially when they don't tell you what love is. That's the problem he has with this general advice. What is love? We all know that there are several kinds of love. First there is passionate romantic love, which has a sexual basis. Then there is motherly love and brotherly love and just simple love that we all have for older people and babies, children and friends. So he thinks we must clarify what we mean by love before we advise someone to love everyone.

Jack's definition is that love is seeing only the good in people concentrating on a person's strengths and ignoring his or her weaknesses. I like that. It takes love out of the emotional, passionate field and puts it into the more rational, logical field of behaviour. For example when a mother shows love for a newborn baby, she can see nothing but the positive. She can't see anything that the baby could do wrong. When the baby develops about one year and starts screaming and wakening her in the middle of the night, slobbering and drooling, her love is replaced by a more realistic type of love. This love encompasses all the baby's behavior, including weaknesses, which the mother now recognizes but still loves her baby with unconditional love.

The same rationale applies when two young people fall madly in love. They see only the good things about their partners. They are blind to each other's limitations and shortcomings. When they live together and begin to notice the failures and weaknesses of one another, the magical love relationship changes to something more realistic. George Bernard Shaw has said that romantic love is a form of temporary madness.

What Jack learns from this is that the kind of love we want to have for everyone we meet is really a form of positive thinking. It means concentrating on what's good about others and overlooking their limitations.

This makes sense to him. If people stop judging and criticizing others and trying to change them and concentrate on their strengths, instead of their weaknesses, it would be a wonderful world. Wouldn't it be great if we knew that every place we go people would be searching for the good in us and trying to overlook our limitations and accepting us as we are? Instead, we find many people looking for our weaknesses and concentrating on those characteristics.

As a general approach to life, Jack says that this attitude of liking people and searching for their good qualities is one of the finest beginnings for good human relations and the development of feeling good. If we demonstrate love for others, we learn how to love more deeply. As we criticize and judge others we become fearful of human relationships.

Everyone we meet will be our antagonist or our supporter depending on what we demonstrate to them. Generally speaking, if we love others, they will love us. If we dislike others, they will dislike us.

One very important aspect of love is that it should be unconditional. For example Jack claims that if you are associated with a person who is hostile and critical, you can dislike what that person is doing, but you will love the person who is doing it. In other words no matter what others do, you will love them but you may dislike what they are doing. This is unconditional love.

According to Jack this applies also to the love of God. At times, you may be critical of the way the world is operating and blame God for this. What you don't realize is that God is making his decisions based on wider knowledge than yours. There may be past lives and future lives that he is considering. No matter what decisions God makes, the spiritual person gives him unconditional love.

Unconditional love also applies to love of you. No matter what bad things you think you have done, don't stop loving yourself. You are a perfect spirit from the universe and as such you deserve unconditional love. You will try to correct your weaknesses.

All the great religions have love as the basis of their teaching. Jesus, Moses, Mother Teresa and Muhammad all taught their followers to love one another and to love themselves as a starting point for being happy. This convinces Jack. If these great spiritual leaders have found that love is important in their philosophy, he will accept it. They have been students of living, students of people and spiritual students. They have observed their followers in action and they have practiced what they preached with great success.

Jack will give you a formula for loving others which you may find difficult to apply at times, but you will find it works in most cases and will enable you to get eustress going with almost anyone with whom you come in contact.

Here is the formula:

- Visualize yourself getting along perfectly with everyone. If you have been in conflict with some person, start to visualize yourself getting along well. In your mind, see yourself meeting with that person and having a congenial relationship.

- If it is someone you know, think about her best qualities. Think of everything she has done right and keep concentrating on those things. If it is someone you don't know, concentrate on the good things you have heard about her and ignore the bad. Praise her about one of her good qualities or good activities if the opportunity to do this is appropriate. Don't criticize her.

- No matter what she is doing or has done. Accept the other person as she is.

- Don't try to change her. Remember she is on her own track and no matter what she does or says it is her way of behaving. Just let her continue in her own way with you watching in awe but not trying to change her in any way.

- Give her unconditional love. Listen to her and ask for her opinions and advice.

- Be of service. Give her anything you can and try to help her. Smile at her.
- Expect nothing in return.
- Don't do this to gain advantages for yourself, but rather to help her.

Most people will respond favorably to this kind of treatment. Jack knows it will be difficult for you to treat people that way especially if they have been abrasive, demanding or hostile. To help you deal with this he will say that this type of behavior on her part means that she is really fearful and insecure and wants love and understanding. Try to visualize her with her hands out stretched asking for help. She is hurting and instead of asking for love and understanding she is lashing out to get your attention.

Try this formula on anyone you are having conflicts with and Jack thinks you will find them changing their attitude towards you when they find you are sending them love instead of criticism.

Some time ago when Jack was putting this formula together, he had an experience which proved to him how effective it is. One afternoon he went into one of our large retail stores in Toronto to buy a suit. Unfortunately, he picked a man who was one of the worst salesmen he had ever seen. He ignored him from the beginning by continuing to talk to one of his friends while Jack was waiting. When Jack asked him where to find a certain type of suit, he pointed vaguely in a direction behind him. After some searching Jack couldn't find the size or type of suit he wanted. When he returned to this man for further instructions, he waved vaguely in the same direction with some impatient mumbled instructions.

Finally, when Jack found the type of suit he wanted and returned to have it fitted he was feeling extremely critical and judgmental and was planning to report this man and try to have him replaced by someone more suitable for this type of work. At that point, Jack thought about his new theory of love and decided to try it. He immediately started visualizing himself getting along better with this salesman and he tried to think of something good about him on which he could concentrate. He couldn't think of anything he did right, so he made up something. As he came out of the fitting booth he smiled and said, "You're a great salesman. What I liked was that you didn't hover over me or try to pressure me to buy something."

In a flash as if by magic, the salesman changed his whole attitude. He said, "Mr. McQuaig, it's a pleasure to do business with you. Here is my card. When you come in to pick up this suit I want you to ask for me so I can be sure you get prompt service. Meanwhile, I am going to do something for you. Normally this suit won't be ready until next Friday, but I'm going to put it ahead on our schedule so you will get it Tuesday instead of Friday." Jack couldn't believe it. His love formula had changed this man into a new and effective salesman and Jack said to himself, "It works." Since then, he has used this method in many situations with great success.

Jack believes we all need to keep reminding ourselves that the greatest needs of people are to feel important and to be understood and loved. If you can give them these things you will build good relationships. One of the best things you can do for people is to agree with them. He doesn't mean by this that you should agree with people when you strongly disagree with them. What he means is that being right is very important to all of us. If you tell a person that they are wrong about something, they look on this as a put down and a questioning of their wisdom and intelligence. So Jack's advice is to avoid open disagreement with others.

If someone says that they don't believe violence and pornography on TV are harmful to young people, and you violently disagree, Jack advises you to try to keep your response under control. Instead of telling this person that they are wrong and questioning their wisdom and judgment you might say, "That's an interesting viewpoint: Why do you believe that these things are not harmful to children?" You have a choice. Do you want to be right or to get along with others and be happy?

Let her talk. You can get your point across in a nice way without telling this person that she is wrong. It's all a matter of tact and diplomacy. Being agreeable with others is vital to developing good relationships. Whenever you feel a conflict building up with your partner, instead of trying to prove that you are right you can stop the disagreement by saying, "You could be right about that." Or "That's an interesting point of view."

Many experts in marital counselling will tell you that the greatest cause of marital discord is when the partners fight over who is right and who is wrong or who knows best. Marriages often break up because the partners are fighting to prove who is right, when sometimes they are both wrong. I personally think the biggest cause of marital discord is being disagreeable. If you always disagree with your partner, you have a constant conflict on your hands. It can start early when the minister says, "Do you take this woman to be your lawfully wedded wife?" and the bridegroom says to himself, "Provided she agrees with me and does what I tell her."

The importance of love and understanding in increasing good relationships is also demonstrated by something that happened in Rosito, Pennsylvania, a small community, which had few heart attacks when compared to adjacent communities.

Rosito had been settled in 1882 by immigrants from southern towns in Italy. These people had close family and friend relationships, which they maintained in Rosito.

This made the environment filled with love, caring and goodwill towards their friends and neighbors. This congenial setting apparently built eustress and protected their health.

Love is so powerful, according to Jack that it is just as important in keeping people physically healthy as is the right food and exercise.

According to Dr. Dean Ornish, in his book, *Love and Survival*, the people in Rosito apparently connected with one another in mind, heart and spirit. Dr. Ornish claims there is a great healing power that comes with connecting, for you and for those with whom you connect. Connecting means spending loving time, having fun together building good relationships, not sitting in front of TV, shopping or driving somewhere. These latter people are just co-existing, not connecting. They are not really together.

Jack claims that you can solve many of your problems and feel good and be successful and happy if you can love yourself. It seems ridiculous that you are spending time, effort and money to try to achieve happiness and success and yet you could have it all, if you could start loving yourself.

Why will this simple change of attitude make a big difference in your life? Jack explains that if you love yourself unconditionally, you will automatically love others unconditionally.

Chapter Fifteen

RELAXING

In this final chapter before I give you the conclusion, Jack's last but not least important thing to remember is that you must learn how to relax. It is imperative and an important element to your good health both mentally and physically. Jack tells us that by learning how to relax, you can keep yourself constantly in a good state, capable of being more at home with yourself and at ease with others and with your environment. With a relaxed approach, you will find yourself moving through life with less friction and distress. People will enjoy your tolerant, easy-going attitude. You will be more capable of dealing with human relations and will be more effective as a leader.

In Jack's research and reading he has discovered that one of the characteristics of the neurotic, is a tendency to overreact to situations and waste energy by being in a state of anger, tension, hostility or suspicion. We all see this when we see people challenging or confronting others. Their face goes red, they speak at a different pitch. Road rage these days is a perfect example of how people get themselves worked up into an unhealthy state and expend negative energy. Mentally healthy people on the other hand, take life in their stride, roll with the punches and do not become overly emotional about situations in which they are involved. They have a relaxed approach to life.

In his human relations work appraising hundreds of key personnel, Jack has noticed that the men and women who are in the best state are usually relaxed people with plenty of patience and a great respect for others and their problems. They allow themselves to relax, to enjoy each moment and to use the moment to its best advantage. In other words, these people keep in a relaxed state while they work and play. As a result they can work longer and play more and enjoy it.

If you are going to follow Jack's advice and model the style of people who are in a good state, you must develop the habit of relaxing, so you will go through life with a minimum of resistance, hostility, impatience and anger.

Jack says that your mental state depends a great deal on your ability to relax while you work and play. When you relax, you will be able to think clearly and be alert and enthusiastic. You will show initiative and be creative and will utilize your physical and mental capacities to the utmost.

The person in a relaxed state may not be working extremely hard but she is working smart, avoiding unnecessary detail and setting priorities. Jack's belief is that if you concentrate on the most important things, you will spend your time planning and setting goals for the near future and the long term.

Jack advises people to learn to relax and be more effective at their work to think ahead and make sure the things they are doing today are the most important things that will not only contribute to immediate goals, but to long term goals.

The person in a relaxed state can patiently study their job to see if better systems and procedures can be developed. This way you are constantly trying to improve the climate where you work and play. You listen to people and learn from their experiences and try to motivate yourself to co-ordinate your efforts with your co-workers. You think hard about how you can improve your own training and development. You show initiative and have the vitality, energy and alertness, to inspire others to try and do what you are doing.

When you are working in a job for which you are suited and which will give you the opportunity for the advancement you want, try to enjoy the actual work you are doing, rather than focusing all your energies on promotion and advancement. Set as your first objective the mastery of your job so you will get the great satisfaction that comes from excellence in your work. You will get into a more relaxed state if you can get pleasure from the work you do.

Jack always reminds me not to take myself too seriously. Remember, Jack would say, Shakespeare called life "a tale told by an idiot." Try to have some fun while you are working and living he tells me. Don't go around wishing you were someone else. Keep developing your sense of humour. Life is a game and we are just some of the players, not the umpires or the referees. Even if we aren't winning we have the right to sit in the stands and eat peanuts.

In Jack's research he found there are a number of theories on the best way to relax. Dr. Edmund Jacobson, M.D., describes a technique of progressive relaxation in his book, *You Must Relax* (McGraw-Hill, New York). According to Dr. Jacobson, every time you use a muscle in your arm or leg or finger, it is tensed by a message from your brain. When any muscle is extremely active, whether because of physical exertion or tension, the nerve leading to that muscle is busy and using energy.

If your muscles are kept in a constant state of tension, your energy is dissipated through overuse. Under continuing pressure, the muscles remain constantly tense. This tension drains your energy whether you are working or playing.

Dr. Jacobson suggest to get rid of this wasteful tension, you must first recognize it. To do this, lie down on your bed, flat on your back. Bend your right hand back at the wrist and hold it in this position until you get a feeling of tension in the muscle on the top side of your right arm which is pulling your hand back. Make sure you feel this tension.

Let your hand drop forward and notice the tension disappear. Or has it completely disappeared? Maybe you can still feel some remaining tension in this muscle although it is not being actively used to move any part of your body. This is wasteful tension and if you can recognize it, practise getting rid of it. Just let that part of your muscle go. Instead of tensing it, try to get it to do nothing, just the opposite of tension, until it becomes relaxed. Practise this for a few minutes.

Try bending your right hand forward at the wrist until you get the feeling of tension in the muscle on the underside of your arm. Discover this tension by pulling your hand backward for a few seconds. Now that you recognize it, try to get rid of this feeling of tension in that particular arm muscle by letting it go.

Lying flat on your back, pull the right forearm up to a vertical position by tensing the large muscle above the elbow.

Try to let go completely with this muscle. Let your arm fall forward and get the feeling that it is lying there useless with the bed supporting it. Practise this for a few minutes. Gradually you will start to develop the habit of relaxation in that large muscle.

Now try lifting up your entire right arm by the shoulder muscles to get the feeling of tension there. Then let your whole arm fall. Let these muscles go and try to get the feeling of relaxation in them. Practice this for a few minutes. Do this with the same muscle in the left arm.

This relaxation can be extended to the legs by tensing and relaxing the various leg muscles in a similar way.

Try to relax the muscles of the face and eyes and jaw. Put an exaggerated frown on your face with extra tension. Now relax the frown and try to get the feeling of relaxation in your facial muscles. Next close your eyes extremely tight, putting tension in the fine muscles around the eyes, now open the eyes normally to get the opposite feeling of relaxation. Practise the same thing with the jaw, and then let your jaw fall open in a relaxed manner. You can do the same tensing and relaxing with the stomach muscles, the chest muscles and the back muscles.

Jack tells me that if you do all of these exercises regularly, trying to get the feeling of tension, then of relaxation throughout all the body muscles and end each time with a few minutes of complete relaxation of each set of muscles, eventually your muscles will develop the habit of relaxing. As one muscle relaxes, it contributes to relaxation in all the others, so each time you get a muscle into the habit of relaxing, you are taking a step forward. I have tried this and it takes practice. Jack has helped me by going over these techniques again and again and encouraging me to keep trying until I have it working for me.

To enhance your relaxed feeling you can also use the sense of hearing to describe your relaxation. Talk to yourself by saying, "I am completely relaxed." "I am letting go of tension," "I am becoming easy-going and completely relaxed."

If you are finding it difficult to relax, you may be trying too hard and making too great an effort. Just try to let go. Relaxation is a condition in your muscles that cannot be forced. It must come about naturally when the muscles let go. If you try to force a muscle to relax, you will build up more tension.

CONCLUSION

Jack McQuaig has been successful in many fields of endeavor and I will try to explain some of his achievements.

His first success was as a psychological consultant. In this business he did appraisals of personnel for corporate managers. Whenever one of his clients was hiring a salesman or a manager, he would send him to Jack's office where he would take psychological tests and be interviewed. This business was very successful and gave Jack the knowledge for his seminars for managers which he later developed.

His most prominent success is in the business world. He has been a successful entrepreneur with three small organizations run by his two sons. Jack often says that he is now retired and is fortunate to have two sons who are running the businesses better than he did.

Probably his second greatest achievement has been to write twelve books. He is still writing and thinks that he may do fifteen books before he retires from writing. His latest books are in the self-help area and he gives his books away in his effort to help others to achieve their goals. He has made little effort to sell his books but great effort to give them to those who need help.

His third greatest achievement is probably the conducting of seminars on management topics all over the USA and

Canada. In the early days of this business activity he was one of the few speakers conducting public programs on management topics. He claims that at one time he was teaching many of America's middle and top managers how to run their businesses.

Another great success for Jack was in his development of psychological tests. One of his psychological measurement instruments, the McQuaig Word Survey, is very helpful in predicting the kind of work a person can do well. The Word Survey has been translated into many languages and is used in corporations all over the world in the selection of personnel.

Jack has always been searching for new ideas and new knowledge. In addition to his Bachelor of Commerce degree from Queens University and his MA in Industrial Psychology from Toronto University, he has taken programs on management from the Barksdale Organization in California, the Neuro Linguistics Company in California and the Tack Organization in London, England. For several years he conducted the Tack Sales Training programs in Canada. This lead to his founding of MICA with his son, Don, which is now one of Canada's largest management training centers.

When he achieved the goal of semi-retirement he turned to the spiritual world for inspiration and wrote the book *On the Path to Spiritual Fitness*. This led to his creation of a new religion called Godliness which doesn't require Jesus or Buddha or any spiritual leader. All it requires is you and God. Jack's book gives the reader the formula for getting to God directly.

He has always had an interest in George Bernard Shaw. This culminated in his appearance as a speaker at the Shaw Festival summer educational program in 1958. Eventually, he wrote a biography of Shaw and a play about Shaw.

In the early days Jack lost money in the stock market but eventually he learned how to trade stocks successfully.

Maybe it is not so unusual to find some person who has been successful in one or two areas but I can only find one other person who has been successful in ten.

Jack has been successful as a psychological consultant, business entrepreneur, psychological test creator, Bernard Shaw biographer, public speaker, seminar leader, and stock market trader. He has written twelve books and created a religion and has two University degrees. One in accounting and a graduate degree in psychology. If you can find anyone with this many achievements, I hope you will contact me because I have searched the business, academic, artistic and spiritual worlds and I can't find anyone who has been as successful in as many fields as Jack, except George Bernard Shaw.

While doing these things, Jack has married Audrey, a wonderful wife to whom he has been married for fifty-eight years. This has resulted in another big success. Five children and ten grand children is quite an achievement.

How did he do all these things without even trying very hard? The answer lies in his open mindedness, willingness to try new things, persistence and positive attitudes.

From the courses he took, he learned many things that helped him. Although at the time he wasn't sure that these ideas were working. For example he was visualizing what he wanted to achieve. He thought that if he visualized something constantly, it would come to pass, and it did.

Among other things he kept affirming that he would be successful and used creative thinking as a helpful technique. Praying, meditating, chanting, reading, relaxing, watching television and using humour also helped him to achieve his goals.

Jack is the first to admit that he got help from acupuncture, shiatsu, massage, reflexology, homeopathic medicine and naturopathic medicine. By keeping an open mind, and listening to any expert that was available and using their ideas in his life he was able to succeed.

Keeping in excellent physical condition by exercising, dieting and having a satisfying life style and by getting into the kind of work he loved also contributed to his success.

Most important of all, according to Jack, is his belief in God and his faith in Gods ability to help him.

JACK'S FINALE

As we come to the end of this book, I wanted to reveal one of Jack's secrets. He is planning a third career. Instead of completely retiring as most people do, he will continue to do what he has been. Praying, meditating and asking for God's help and visualizing himself living to 110 years old. But adding two more elements.

One: In the financial area he wants to accumulate five million dollars which he can use to help the underprivileged. In the physical area he wants to play golf in the seventies. In the spiritual area, he wants to open his own church.

Yes, he wants a church where he can establish his religion of Godliness. Here he will install a minister in one half of the building. This half will also have three hundred pews. In the other half of the building will be Jack's office and the offices of those who are administering the work of his church.

On the outside of the church will be a sign reading,

"The adherents of Jack McQuaig's religion of Godliness will meet here every Sunday morning at 11:00 am."

Jack's philosophy is that dying will be a pleasant experience. He will enjoy it. He will also enjoy going to heaven where he will be very happy being thirty years old, enjoying a temperature of 70 degrees and not needing a car because he will be able to fly. In heaven he will live in a big mansion with a number of volunteer helpers. Here he will be re-united with his family and friends.

Here he will practice his psychology of helping people to solve their problems.

QUESTIONS AND ANSWERS

We have covered a lot of topics in the previous chapters. When Jack speaks publicly, he always has a question and answer period following his presentation. Here are a few questions that have been asked of him. I hope you will find them of value and I encourage you to send in your questions once you have read this book.

Q: At what age did you start your program of dieting and exercising and why did you start?

A: I was age 22 when I started this program. I did it to improve my health because I had been sick. I also read a book by Dr. Robert A. Jackson, which motivated me to start a fitness program. The title of the book was *How to be always well*.

Q: Have you ever been tempted to give up your efforts to keep in good health and if not, what do you feel has been the most positive factor in this?

A: No. I never thought of giving up my fitness program. The reason? It was helping me to feel good and have more energy.

Q: Over the years, you must have encountered some difficulties or disabilities that have prevented you from doing the things you like. Can you tell us what they have been and how you have overcome them?

A: Yes, I have had one situation where I suffered a rhythmic heart disability. This slowed me down for about a month. Getting plenty of rest, exercise and the proper diet and using my relaxing techniques helped me to recover. My doctors told me there was something wrong with my heart but they couldn't find out what it was. Their advice was to lead a relaxed, easy going life. I don't try to protect my heart by taking it easy and don't push myself. I just try to lead a normal life.

Q: Were you always as giving as you are now, or is this something that has come with experience and age?

A: I have always had some tendency to give. It has also increased over the years so I definitely get more satisfaction now from giving than receiving.

Q: In these previous chapters I found that a large factor in your success was the fact that you have always been persistent. Do you feel this was a trait of your parents or was it something self taught?

A: My mother was an extremely persistent person and I may have inherited this tendency from her. However I tried to be more persistent as I matured and realized how important persistence was for success. My father was more casual and took life easy. My grandparents on my father's side were both very persistent and lived to be in their late eighties.

Q: In times of extreme adversity, what is it you turn to first? Praying, Meditating, Chanting or affirming?

A: I would say a combination of all but meditation is beyond a doubt my most powerful help when I am in trouble.

Q: What was it that drove you to write your first book?

A: I wasn't driven to write it but I was urged to write my first book by Frederdrik Fell, my first publisher.

Q: With all your businesses how did you have time to write?

A: I wrote when I had a break from work. In the beginning I did most of my writing on buses, trains, subways and airplanes. Eventually I set aside half an hour in the evening and half an hour before work for writing.

Q: If you have to choose just one of your possible occupations which one would it be?

A: Writing of course. I love to write because it makes me think and be creative. To me it is a fun activity, particularly when I produce a book or an article of which I am proud.

Q: You have a very large family and I know they all support what you have done in the past and what you are currently doing. How do each of your family members contribute to your success and happiness and how do they differ?

A: This is too big a question to answer here. But briefly I

would say that they have all contributed to my success. Linda and Wendy in writing. Don and Peter in administration and John in humour.

Q: What situation in the past 10 years would you say exhibited the most spiritual reaction out of you?

A: At my golf club we had a table in the coffee shop where ten of us gathered together for lunch almost every day. One by one these men died until I was the only one left. This called for a lot of spiritual thinking and acting on my part.

Q: Everyone gets upset. How do you cope with situations where you have not acted spiritually and how have you overcome these?

A: One time I was playing golf with my wife on a nine hole golf course. Two men who were better players than us kept pushing up behind us and asked to play through. For some reason I didn't like their style and kept blocking them from playing through in spite of the fact that my wife kept urging me to let them play through. This taught me to be more relaxed in my behaviour and to be more concerned abut helping others.

Q: Several of your methods of diet and advice from professionals cost a lot of money. What do you recommend for those people who do not have the funds to see alternative physicians?

A: I recommend that they go to the library and look up books on exercising, dieting and spirituality and follow what these books are recommending and use their general ideas as much as possible. They could start with the books of Dr. Deepak Chopra and Dr. Wayne Dyer.

Q: Your clubs are fabulous sounding, but it is very expensive to join these clubs. Do you have any suggestions for those who are not members of clubs?

A: Yes, some could afford a cheaper organization like the YMCA. Others could find a coffee shop close to where they live and hang out there whenever they want to socialize. Churches and bars are other organizations that welcome people who want to make friends and socialize.

Q: How were you able to maintain your health program when you travelled as extensively as you have?

A: It wasn't easy. I did my exercises in my hotel room and I was very selective in the food I ordered and very picky in what I ate. I kept constantly thinking of my exercise program and walked up and down in airports, train stations and bus depots when waiting for transportation.

Q: Your mother seems to have been a great influence on you. Can you tell me a little about how you feel she helped shape your mind and future?

A: Right you are. In the early days up until I was twenty one my mother supported me in nearly everything I wanted to do, playing hockey and tennis and baseball, dating many different girls and loaning me the family car when I needed transportation.

Most of all she urged me to continue my education

and loaned me the money I needed to go to University. Fortunately I kept track of everything and was able to pay her back.

Q: You have spoken about a neighbour of yours that you thought was quite spiritual – I recall you telling the story of you being with him and you got into a fender bender. You thought you would see a real spiritualist in action but to your surprise he became hostile. Can you recall this story for me and tell me how it made you feel about spirituality at that time?

A: You have described this situation very well. This man was a big shot in his church where he held high offices. When we came out of a restaurant one night after having dinner a man hit his car and damaged it slightly. He was very hostile with the man and gave him a lecture on proper behaviour and driving skills.

This convinced me that all people who pretend to be spiritual do not act in a spiritual manner

Q: You have told us that you have always resorted to meditation to help you through the difficult times. Can you tell us what was the most difficult situation that you have had to overcome?

A: The most difficult situation for me to overcome was when ten of my golfing partners all died and left me alone at our luncheon table. Meditation was my best help to keep me from distress.

Q: Of all your clubs can you tell me which is your favorite

and how it has helped you over the years, in different ways?

A: I like all of my clubs but I think the Toronto Arts and Letters club is my favorite. Here I have met people from the artistic world who have been very helpful to me. As Chairman of the Writers Table, I have been given some responsibility and have enjoyed helping many people who were trying to write books.

Q: You have been extremely successful. People management has been one of your successes. Have you ever had difficulties with staffing and how did you overcome the problems?

A: Yes, in spite of my psychological tests and my skill at interviewing, I have made a few mistakes in hiring. I had to fire one man because he didn't succeed in his job and he disagreed with our philosophy of appraisal.

Another man was not very strong in his job and I had to spend more time with him trying to motivate him to work harder and follow company policy.

MARNI'S FINAL THOUGHTS

As near as I have been able to appraise him here is the way Jack thinks.

He doesn't try to change how God is running the world but tries to adjust to it.

He believes that he can get whatever he wants by asking for God's help and by visualizing it. He thinks positively about everything and believes he can make things happen his way.

Meanwhile he uses many techniques to make things go the way he wants. He prays, meditates, affirms, chants and analyses his intuitional thoughts. He also sets goals for what he wants to achieve. As a result he has very good control of his life.

Instead of constantly striving for more things, more power and more skills, he concentrates on enjoying what he has. He is grateful for everything God has given him.

He is positive, optimistic and enthusiastic about his life. I have often heard him say that it isn't what happens to you that causes most of your unhappiness but how you think about what is happening to you. If you keep thinking positively you can feel good in circumstances that are bad for you. It's the thoughts that are influential.

Most important of all is his belief in God and the spiritual. In every important decision he makes he asks himself, "What would the spiritual person do in this situation? What would God want me to do?"

Books by Jack H. McQuaig

How to Pick Men
Frederick Fell Inc.

How to Motivate Men
Frederick Fell Inc.

How to Interview and Hire Productive People
(with Peter L. and Donald H. McQuaig)
Frederick Fell Inc.

Challenge Yourself and Live
General Publishing

Your Business, Your Son and You
B. Klein Publications

The Pregnant Male
Hunter Carlyle Publishing

Synergy and the Power of Personal Proficiency
Hunter Carlyle Publishing

Like Yourself and Live
Hunter Carlyle Publishing

Keep Feeling Good with Mental Fitness
Hunter Carlyle Publishing

Improve Your Golf Game with Spirituality
Hunter Carlyle Publishing

ISBN 142515913-3